Footprints
in the

DUE DATE			
3/4/05			
			Printed in USA

Footprints in the Snow

More Stories about God's Mysterious Ways

Catherine Marshall
Annie Johnson Flint
Arthur Gordon
& others

DIMENSIONS

FOR LIVING

NASHVILLE

FOOTPRINTS IN THE SNOW
First Dimensions for Living edition 1992

This book is printed on recycled, acid-free paper.

Library of Congress Cataloging-in-Publication Data

Footprints in the snow / [contributors include] Annie Johnson Flint, Arthur Gordon, Catherine Marshall, and others.
    p. cm.
    ISBN 0-687-13253-3 (alk. paper)
    1. Providence and government of God. 2. Christian biography—United States. I. Marshall, Catherine, 1914-
BT96.2.F66   1992
231.7—dc20   92-7548
                                                                CIP

All Scripture quotations, unless otherwise noted, are from the King James or Authorized Version of the Bible.

Scripture quotations marked RSV are from the Revised Standard Version of the Bible, copyright 1946, 1952, 1971 by the Division of Christian Education of the National Council of the Churches of Christ in the United States of America and are used by permission.

Scripture quotations marked NIV are from the New International Version of the Bible, copyright © 1978 by New York International Bible Society, and are used by permission.

Scripture quotations marked TLB are from *The Living Bible*, copyright 1971 owned by transfer to Illinois Marine Bank N.A. (as trustee). Used by permission of Tyndale House Publisher, Wheaton, IL 60188.

Scripture quotations marked NEB are from *The New English Bible*, copyright © 1976 by the Delegates of the Oxford University Press and the Syndics of the Cambridge University Press, and are used by permission.

Every attempt has been made to credit the sources of copyrighted material used in this book. If any such acknowledgment has been inadvertently omitted or miscredited, receipt of such information would be appreciated.

Except as noted below, and for some poems, all material is reprinted from *Guideposts* magazine. Copyright © 1948, 1959, 1963, 1968, 1970, 1971, 1974, 1976, 1977, 1978, 1982, 1983, 1985, 1986, 1987, 1988, 1989, 1990 by Guideposts Associates, Inc., Carmel, NY 10512.

"Return from Tomorrow" by George C. Ritchie, Jr., is copyright © 1963 by Dr. George C. Ritchie, Jr., and is reprinted by permission.

The poem "When I Am Sore Beset" by Antoinette Goetschius is used by permission of *Decision* magazine.

MANUFACTURED IN THE UNITED STATES OF AMERICA

Contents

Preface

Efrem Zimbalist, Jr.'s first musical composition, based on Psalm 150, was going to be performed in Merion, Philadelphia. It was 1953, and he had just bought four new tires for the motorized love of his life—a 1934 Packard. What could go wrong? Everything! Four flat tires on one car in one day is hard to believe, but it happened. When the fourth one blew on the Henry Hudson Parkway, he was a dangerous man. Not even the rain could cool him off. No one would stop to help—that is, not until a mysterious white-haired man pulled up behind him in an old jalopy. Only years later, after he had drawn closer to God, would Efrem know the meaning of that day's events.

Phyllis rarely had time to play the piano, so she indulged herself in piano playing when she and the boys visited her parents. This time she took a pile of long-neglected sheet music with her—some of her favorites and some she knew her father would enjoy. How amazed she was when her father asked her to play some ragtime tunes and she actually could play them—*and play them well*. There was no way for her to know the shock that lay ahead.

Sandy knew that guide dogs have to be walked regularly, so she and her California-bred guide dog, Dustin, left their warm Long Island apartment and walked out into the snowstorm. This was Dustin's first snowstorm, and he was a bit confused. Forty-five harrowing minutes later, they finally made it back. A friend suggested that next time they ask the Lord to go with them. So when it was time for another walk, Sandy prayed for the Lord's guidance and then gave Dustin a command that a blind person gives only when another person is leading the way. Dustin perked up and headed off as if he knew exactly where to go. How surprised Sandy would be when a stranger would ask about the extra set of footprints upon their return.

Many of us have seen "footprints in the snow"—evidence of the ordinary and extraordinary ways God mysteriously impacts our lives and reassures us that we are not subject to mere chance but are part of a divine design. These moments offer dramatic proof of God's active and personal love for us.

This is a collection of "footprints in the snow." These true stories of God's transforming power and constant love are told by persons who have experienced firsthand God's active presence in their lives. Like the stories in *Snowflakes in September*, the awe-inspiring accounts in this second volume of stories about God's mysterious ways call us to a renewed and wonder-filled faith.

God moves in ways we cannot always understand. May the wonder and joy of God's mystery enable you to see and celebrate the "footprints in the snow."

GOD

Utters

HIS VOICE

Whether you turn to the right or to the left, your ears will hear a voice behind you, saying, "This is the way; walk in it."

—ISAIAH 30:21, NIV

God is our refuge and strength, a very present help in trouble. . . . The heathen raged, the kingdoms were moved; he uttered his voice, the earth melted. The Lord of hosts is with us.

—PSALM 46:1, 6–7

FOUR BIG LITTLE WORDS
—*Ivar Seger*

> *Trust* in the Lord for His promise is true,
> *Delight* in the Lord, it will bring joy to you.
> *Commit* yourself, do His will every day,
> *Wait* on the Lord, hear what He has to say.

GOD DOES SPEAK TO US
Marion Bond West

Of course, God doesn't tap you on the shoulder and exhort you like your boss, in deep, commanding tones. No, He makes Himself known in various ways. Here's how I came to learn to make myself available to Him.

I never wanted anything in life but to be a wife and mother. I believed this was my calling. When I married Jerry, it all came true for me. By 1968 I was the mother of two young girls and infant twin boys. All four were active and demanding. Suddenly I was up to my ears in diapers and formula and laundry; some days I was so harried and dragged out I never got out of my bathrobe.

Jerry and I were both believers, and when I got the children dressed and we trooped off to church each Sunday, we looked like a picture-book family. We were, except for me. I was drained—running on empty. I began to resent that Jerry went off to work all week to an interesting job with people he enjoyed while I endured daily bedlam at home.

On the morning of March 4, 1972, I told Jerry, "I've got to be alone for a while. Please take the children."

"Sure, sure," he said brightly. "I understand. Maybe it'll cheer you up."

"That's easy for you to say," I said through clenched teeth. Jerry got the message. He quickly collected the children and packed them outside to the yard. It's fortunate he did or I might have screamed at him. I was screaming inside.

I felt like a failure as a wife, mother, and person. I went into the den, shut the door, and whimpered, "Help, Lord, please help me. Take over, I can't do it anymore. There's got to be something more for me in life."

I stood stock still. I wasn't absolutely sure what I was doing. But I listened. Oh, how I *listened.*

And then I began to feel something, a feeling of warmth. I felt a love so intense that it seemed to fill and overflow me and permeate the den and reverberate throughout the whole house. . . .

I didn't need to hear words; I could sense Jesus saying, *I've waited a long time for you to do this. I'm pleased and I'm going to help you. I love you.* Although I didn't see anything visible, I knew that Jesus was with me now in a way that He'd never been before, and I felt He was smiling. I smiled back. I'd almost forgotten how to smile. I wondered how I had sung "And He walks with me, and He talks with me, and He tells me I am His own"* almost all my life at church and never once heard Him "say" anything to me before.

Shortly after that experience, I began thinking more and more about my writing—maybe I should write a book. The idea kept returning. Could it be that God was instructing me to write a book?

"I can't," I told Him. "I don't have the time or energy or know-how. I have four small children. I can't even spell. You know how tired I am after the children are asleep. My typewriter is ancient. I want to, but . . . Tell you what, Lord. You know that nice editor lady at *Guideposts* who writes me the encouraging rejection letters, Dina Donohue? Well, if she were to write in her next letter (if there is another letter) 'Dear Marion' instead of 'Dear Mrs. West,' I'd know You were speaking and telling me to write a book . . . and I'd do it."

A letter from Dina Donohue (another rejection) arrived that week. I was standing at our mailbox waiting and looking for it. I read it still standing by the box: "Dear Marion, I cannot call you Mrs. West any longer, for I know you far too well." I

---

*"In The Garden," by C. Austin Miles, © 1912, 1940 by the Rodeheaver Company.

laughed, cried, jumped up and down in the yard, and ran around in a joyful circle as my astonished children gaped.

"God wants me to write a book!" I fairly screamed to them and the neighbors. No one in the world, no theology, no argument, no logic could have convinced me that The God of the Universe had not spoken directly to *me!* It was a long road, but my first book was published four years later.

Sometimes, even as I have learned to listen for God's voice ("My soul, wait thou only upon God," Psalm 62:5), there have been long, dark, almost unbearable times when He didn't speak—or at least I didn't hear Him. When discouraging silence prevailed, I learned that there were always such verses as John 14:18: "I will not leave you comfortless," and Psalm 147:3: "He heals the brokenhearted" (RSV), and many more definite promises. I had to *choose* to stand on them and *believe* them no matter what—as if they were being written for me today.

Once when I was having trouble connecting with God, I asked Him, "Why is it so difficult?" No answer came. Months passed. One night I picked up a book to get my mind off the threatening depression I sensed I'd be facing the next day. Then five words by Oswald Chambers suddenly seemed almost to leave the printed page and invade my defeated spirit like a conquering army rushing to the rescue: "All noble things are difficult."** I sat straight up in bed reasoning: *If all noble things are difficult . . . then I must be doing something noble!* Almost instantly the suffocating depression was lifting. But then I thought, *Why get so excited over five words? Millions of people read this book.* I tuned this out. Belief is for those who want to believe. I had heard from God. I went to sleep savoring, rejoicing in those five words.

Shortly after I began "hearing" from God, Jerry's and my old argument about breakfast resurfaced. Or maybe it was I who argued. Jerry only asked that I cook breakfast, but I hated messing up the kitchen early in the morning. One night after my prayers but before drifting off to sleep, I sensed the words *Cook breakfast for your husband* flashing across my mind.

***My Utmost for His Highest,* by Oswald Chambers, © 1935 by Dodd, Mead & Company.

When I turned to Jerry I saw he was still awake, so I told him, "Jerry, I'm cooking you a good breakfast in the morning." He was so excited that he woke up all during the night wanting to know if it was morning yet. That dutiful obedience put a longed-for new spark in our marriage. Over breakfast Jerry looked at me as if we were dating again. Blessings always follow obedience.

So many times I haven't understood at all why God "told" me to do something, except in retrospect. At another low point in my life God seemed to be telling me to help a quadriplegic: *Teach him to paint.*

"Look," I said, "I can barely paint myself. How can I teach him?" I protested all the way to the hospital where I did volunteer work. When I got to the man's room, he was strapped on a Stryker frame, face down, with his back to me. *This is absurd,* I thought, but I did as God told me and said to the back of his head, "Hi, would you like to learn to paint?"

"Yep. When do we start?" That was in the days before Joni Eareckson had made mouth painting a nationally known technique. I had nothing to go on except instructions from God. The young man began to paint marvelous pictures with a brush held in his teeth. They were framed free of charge by a business-man who recognized his talent. An article about him appeared in the paper. He learned to type by tapping keys with a wand held in his teeth, and went on to lead a full life. How could I stay depressed after I had witnessed a young man make a new life for himself like that?

God's voice is gentle, never pushy. Even when He spoke to me years ago as I stood frying chicken for supper and a danger-ous situation was at hand, His voice was calm. I kept "hearing," *Go find your boys. Now.* Finally, I went, hands still covered in flour, to look for them. I thought, *How silly to stop cooking just to look for the boys.* I found Jon and Jeremy in the washroom. Jeremy was crouched in the dryer with the door shut, wearing a space helmet. Jon was about to blast him off into outer space by pushing the "on" button.

There have been times when I've misunderstood God's mes-sages. But even the biblical Samuel missed God's voice a couple of times. However, Samuel was willing to learn to listen. The third time God spoke to Samuel, he answered, "Speak, Lord; for thy servant heareth" (1 Samuel 3:9). I think God just wants us to be willing to learn to *listen* and that He is pleased when we fully *expect* Him to speak. John 10:27 says, "My sheep hear my voice, and I know them, and they follow me," and in Isaiah 30:21 it says, "And thine ears shall hear a word behind thee, saying, This is the way, walk ye in it." Ezekiel 12:25 says, "For I am the Lord: I will speak." I believe God likes to speak. But there are times when I goof. I blow it. Later, when I realize my mistake, I confess, "I'm sorry, Father. Forgive me. I was wrong."

It's all right, child. I know you want to hear from Me. That's all I want. Keep listening. Expecting Me to speak. Don't tune Me out. You are making remarkable progress. I long to tell you so much more.

"Speak, Lord, for Thy servant is listening."

 ## "THE POOR OLD STRANDED WRECK"

Arthur Gordon

Many summers ago, when I was a youngster growing up in Georgia, we had a cottage at the beach. Life there was pretty casual: no church of our denomination, no TV, no radio. So after supper on Sunday nights we had a family custom of singing hymns.

I hadn't thought of this for years, until the other day when my friend Andrew came back from a trip to California. "Met a fellow out there," he said, "who asked me to give you a message. His name was Charlie and he said he used to be a friend of yours. His message was just one word: Thanks."

"Sure," I said, "I remember Charlie. His family had a cottage near ours at the beach. But what was he thanking me for?"

"Well," Andy said, "Charlie remembers singing hymns at your house on Sunday nights. And he remembers one in particular about shipwrecks."

"Yes," I said, a bit surprised, "there was an old hymn called 'Pull for the Shore, Sailor.' "

"Some years ago Charlie got into trouble with alcohol. Big trouble. He lost his job, lost just about everything. Then one night, sitting in a bar, he heard a voice speak to him. He looked all around, but no one was nearby. First the voice called his name. Then it said, strong and clear, 'Leave the poor old stranded wreck, and pull for the shore!' Charlie sat up straight. He was hearing a command. He got up and walked out of the bar and hasn't touched liquor since. He knew who the stranded wreck was."

 ## WITHOUT KNOWING WHY

Shirley and Terry Law as told to Elizabeth Sherrill

Shirley's story:

The orange juice was already poured, the oatmeal nearly cooked, and I was stirring the scrambled eggs, when the crazy thought popped into my mind.

Take the kids to breakfast at McDonald's.

At first I ignored it. I'd been warned by other young widows that your mind plays tricks on you, living alone. I hadn't really been alone since my husband's death in April 1984, six months earlier—but the children were only six and four.

Go to McDonald's.

The thought came more urgently, and for a second I wondered if I was cracking up. But surely the time for that would have been those two-and-a-half years of watching my tall, blond, athletic young husband die inch by inch of a brain tumor.

If grief hadn't been able to destroy my sanity, I thought, mainly to keep my mind off this silly McDonald's notion, money worries might have. Jim had been a stockbroker here in Tulsa, Oklahoma, operating on commission, which stopped when he could no longer work.

I'd found a job selling Visa and MasterCard services to Tulsa businesses. It kept me out in the car a lot, and I'd cried a lot, there in the car. If I'd been going to fall apart, that would surely have been the time, with everything seemingly against us. Even the washing machine broke down, with no money to repair it, so that in the evening after working and cooking and caring for Jim and mowing the lawn, I'd have to drive out to the Laundromat.

Without faith in God, I thought as I gave the eggs a final turn, I really might have gone crazy. I'd carried a Bible in the car; when I felt panic rise I'd pull over and read and pray until I could go on.

The oatmeal was ready too. In the living room the kids were watching the Saturday morning cartoons. "Marie! Jason!" I called. "Wash your hands and come to the table."

And still something inside my head, quite independent of my own thoughts, was insisting that we were to leave this good hot meal right where it was, get in the car, and drive a mile away to a fast food outlet. I'd never in my life eaten breakfast at McDonald's! Where could such a notion be coming from?

Where indeed . . . ? From the bathroom I heard Marie and Jason splashing water on the floor. I stood there at the stove, spatula in hand, thinking back to a chill December day almost two years before. Wondering if the nudging in my head now was in any way like the nudging that had come to me then . . .

For a week I had been giving Jim and the children cold cereal because the stove, like the washing machine, had broken down, and Jim could no longer trust himself to try electrical repairs. We were three months behind on the house payments, and as for Christmas—Santa just wasn't going to find our chimney.

All that winter morning I had called on potential clients without success. As always when our situation threatened to overwhelm me, I'd pulled the car to the side of the road. And there God spoke to me as clearly as though He'd used audible words: *Will you trust Me, Shirley? For Jim, for the children, now and forever?*

I wanted to—oh, how I wanted to! But where could I get that kind of faith? Certainly I couldn't work it up on my own. "Father," I whispered, "give me that trust."

At once a kind of peace seemed to enter the car. And into that peace dropped the names of three local restaurants. I called on all of them that afternoon and signed on three new accounts.

From then on, these "impressions" came often, sometimes

about work, sometimes about Jim's medication or about one of the children, until I learned to recognize them by a quality of loving urgency very unlike my ordinary thinking process.

This idea in my head now—if it had been anything except "Go to McDonald's," I would have said this was one of those times. But that was too ridiculous!

Wasn't it?

Marie and Jason scrambled into their chairs, still in pajamas on this one morning of the week when we could loaf around the house. Well, we could go to the drive-through window . . .

"Get your bathrobes on," I told them. "We're going to bring breakfast home from McDonald's."

"Yay!" shouted four-year-old Jason. "Can we get French fries?"

But Marie, two years older, looked from the waiting food to me, her face as bewildered as I felt.

Not the drive-through. Go inside to eat.

"On second thought," I called as the kids headed for their rooms, "let's put our clothes on and eat there."

"Boy," I heard Marie tell her brother, "does Mommy ever change her mind."

Twenty minutes later I was steering through Tulsa's Saturday traffic, as baffled as ever as to why we were doing this, when Marie burst into tears. "McDonald's makes me think of Daddy," she sobbed.

Jason was too young to remember the days when Jim could still drive and used to take the two of them out. But he wasn't too young to understand sorrow. "Don't cry, Marie," he said.

"Why don't we pray about it?" I interrupted. So we did, and then Marie said, "God's going to give us a new daddy."

"And someone who loves God," added Jason.

I said nothing. Not out loud. But inwardly I was crying, *No!* No one could replace Jim. Not ever. It wasn't that I was mourning, exactly. I'd done that during the years of seizures and pain. Death had come as such a release for Jim that I'd had to release him too. It was just that I wasn't ready to open again to that kind of total involvement.

Before he died, Jim had asked me to remarry. "You're young, Shirley. You have your whole life ahead of you. Promise me you'll find someone else—when I'm gone."

But I don't want "someone else"! I protested inwardly as I pulled into the crowded McDonald's lot.

As I'd feared, on a Saturday morning there were long lines at the counter. Thinking ruefully of the eggs congealing in the skillet at home, I inched forward while the kids raced around the playground outside. At last I carried our trays to a window table.

That's where we were sitting when they came in, a stocky curly-haired man with a round, pleasant face—probably in his early forties—and three children, ages maybe twelve to five. I recognized the father at once: Terry Law, director of a singing group I'd seen on Oral Roberts's TV program. Certainly no one I knew personally. And yet . . . the unmistakable "impression" came as I watched the four of them get into line at the counter:

This is the reason you are here.

These four people! This particular group, of all the parents and children jamming the restaurant at this moment?

I went on eating, but the food stuck in my throat. Two years' experience in trusting God was insisting, *Introduce yourself.* When I looked up they were setting their trays down at the very next table.

Lord, I objected silently, *he doesn't know me! I can't just say, "Hello, I'm Shirley."*

Then I remembered that a girl I'd known when I was growing up back in Portland, Oregon, had joined Terry Law's music group, Living Sound, several years ago. I could ask Mr. Law about Paula.

He seemed sort of startled to have me speak to him. Paula had married a young man from Living Sound, he said, and together they were pastoring a church in Alaska. He was still looking at me oddly. Probably wondering why I was butting in on the one day he had with his family. More details about his work were coming back to me. Living Sound traveled all over the world, especially behind the Iron Curtain, where young people turned out by the thousands to hear contemporary music with a Christian message. He must hate to have strangers break into his precious time at home.

Just being polite, no doubt, he asked some questions too. When I'd come to Tulsa from Portland, what the kids' names were, what my husband did.

"Jim died last spring," I said. "I'm a widow." Mr. Law set down his coffee container so hard it slopped over. He mopped it up quickly, said he was sorry about Jim, and wrote down my phone number to give to a lawyer he thought could be helpful. Then with an apology he turned back to the youngsters who were clamoring for his attention.

What in the world, I wondered as Marie and Jason and I went out to our car, had flustered him so? And what, for that matter, I thought as I cleared away the cold remains of our uneaten breakfast back at home, had this whole strange episode of dashing out to McDonald's been all about?

I wasn't really expecting God to tell me. I'd learned to trust Him these past two years, not to understand Him. The trusting is everything: it's peace and joy and security long before the answers come. We see only a step at a time, so He can't usually tell us why.

Except that, in this case, He did . . .

Terry's story:
The conversation with Don Moen occurred on a Monday. Don was music director of our organization, Living Sound, and as usual he and I were aboard an airplane. This particular September day in 1984 we were returning from Arizona to our base in Tulsa, Oklahoma.

Our "base"—that's how I thought of Tulsa now: the place we traveled from. Not "home," not since my wife, Jan, died, even though our three beautiful kids were there, and my mother, who'd come down from Canada to care for Misty and Scot and Rebecca.

Across the aisle of the airplane, Don was watching me. "It's two years this month, Terry," he said, as though reading my thoughts.

Two years since my world had changed in as long as it takes for a car to leave the road and crash into a ditch. I'd been far away in England when it happened. No one ever knew what caused the accident. Perhaps the afternoon sun was directly in Jan's eyes on that east-west Oklahoma road.

I only knew that my life seemed to have ended along with hers. I plunged into a bottomless despair, unable to pray or work or believe that I would ever do these things again.

It was in this mood that I went to see my friend and mentor Oral Roberts. Three months before I lost Jan, Oral had lost a son. "How do you keep going?" I asked him.

"I do it," he said, "by praising God."

Praise? When everything in me wanted to cry and curse? "I didn't say feel it," Oral said. "It is simply a fact that God is very great. Tell Him so."

As Oral predicted, praise was the road back into life. Hollow and mechanical at first, it soon became genuine. Praise for Jan. For the thirteen years we'd had together. For her faith. For knowing for sure that she was right now with Jesus.

Week by week the praise grew stronger—and so did my ability to do the things which at first had seemed impossible: to make plans, to travel, to minister to others around the world. Only the loneliness did not change. Praise helped me to live with the emptiness; it did not fill it.

Friends asked, of course, if I would consider marrying again. I knew I should, for the kids' sake. Eleven, nine, and four—how much they needed a mother!

I knew I should consider it for my mom's sake too. No one could have stepped in more selflessly than she had. But she'd raised her family. In justice she should be taking it easy now.

And yet . . . to consider marrying was just what I could not do. Every time I took my loneliness to God, He seemed to tell me: *two years.* It was always the same. I was not even to let the subject enter my head before that time. And that's what I'd told these friends.

Don was leaning across the narrow airplane aisle. "Two years," he repeated. "Remember what you said?"

"That I couldn't think about marrying for two years," I said. "And I haven't."

"Well, two years are up," Don persisted. "You'd better start thinking."

I leaned my head back in the seat, turning over my not-very-hopeful position. To me my three children were the greatest in the world, but what woman would want to take on marriage and motherhood all at once?

Where, for that matter, would I even meet an unmarried woman my own age? There were plenty of single girls in Living Sound, but they were kids in their twenties. I was forty-one.

I'd want someone I could talk to. Someone who could understand the trauma that Misty and Scot and Rebecca had gone through.

I kept waiting for Don to pick up a magazine or something, but from the other side of the aisle he was regarding me expectantly.

"She'd have to be a widow," I heard myself say. "Someone who had as good a marriage as Jan and I had, and knows what it is to lose the most important person in your life. Anyhow," I finished, embarrassed at this outburst, "I don't know any widows."

"God does," Don said. "Let's pray about it."

"I will," I promised him, trying to close off a subject I wasn't ready for.

But Don had bowed his head. "Father, You know Terry's need, and his children's need. We believe You have a plan already at work . . ."

I glanced self-consciously at the other passengers. "Father," I joined in, keeping my voice as low as I could, "there's a widow somewhere who—"

"There's a widow in *Tulsa*," Don corrected.

"All right. In Tulsa. I ask that in Your own time—"

"Quickly."

"Okay. I ask that You quickly reveal . . ."

We prayed for several minutes, there on opposite sides of the aisle, I in generalities, Don in specifics. At the close, he stuck out his hand. With another nervous glance around, I reached across and gripped it.

"Thank You, Father," he pronounced, "that it's done."

Just like that. Prayer, in Don's view, didn't have to be long and eloquent. Just concrete and totally trusting.

At the office in Tulsa a number of crises were waiting for us. Living Sound had teams on the road both in the United States and Europe, including several Iron Curtain countries, and the week was hectic.

Crises or no, however, Saturdays belonged to the family. This was the morning, when I was home, that I took the kids out to breakfast. And the outing always started with a debate.

"Grandy's," I suggested as we piled into the car, naming the place that made the pancakes I liked.

"Denny's," thirteen-year-old Misty voted.

"McDonald's," said six-year-old Rebecca.

"You just like the slide," Scot scoffed with the sophistication of just-turned-eleven. "I say Denny's."

"Denny's wins!" cried Misty.

"Now wait a minute, you two," I said. "Rebecca hasn't gotten to choose for weeks. Let's let her decide today."

And that was how, a few minutes later, the four of us were standing in the line at the McDonald's counter and I was gazing across the room at one of the most beautiful women I'd ever seen. Not a brunette beauty like Jan. This girl had hair the color of sunlight. In fact, where she sat at the window with two little tow-headed kids, the sun streaming through her long blond curls seemed to light up the room.

Maybe it was because I hadn't thought about marriage at all for two years, but I felt a stab of envy for her husband. I was thinking that it would be great just to sit near someone that pretty when, as we left the counter with our trays, the table next to her opened up.

I was trying to decide how to strike up a conversation when to my surprise she did it for me: "Aren't you Terry Law?" A friend of hers, it turned out, had sung for a while with Living Sound. We talked about her friend and then about anything I could think of. I found out that her kids were named Marie and Jason. Their mother's voice was as nice to listen to as her face was to look at.

I peeled the lid from my coffee container as I thought of more questions. Like, "What does your husband do?"

When the girl with golden hair said, "I'm a widow," I took a swallow that scalded my throat all the way down.

What else I said to her I can't remember, except that I managed to get her phone number with some excuse about a lawyer. All I could hear was Don Moen's prayer on the airplane only five days earlier.

All I could think was, *O Lord my God, You are very great.*

Editor's Note: Shirley and Terry were married in January 1985, five months after the "chance" meeting at McDonald's. A sixth child, Laurie Ann Law, was born in March 1986, "but she's not 'ours' any more than all the rest."

ANSWERS

—*Helen Inwood*

Answers to prayers
Come in various ways,
Sometimes in minutes,
Sometimes in days.
And some take years
To fully unfold
The harvest of love
And blessings they hold.

Answers to prayers
Come in various forms,
Sometimes in sunlight,
Sometimes through storms.
Some blossom early
And some blossom late
But each one will flower—
Have faith and wait!

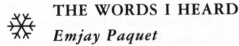

THE WORDS I HEARD

Emjay Paquet

By the summer of 1977, my heavy drinking had taken its toll. I
was alone, and the only creature in the world that I cared about
was my Burmese cat, Chocolate Mousse. One July day I had
locked myself out of my apartment. The neighbor who helped
me get in not only dried my boozy tears, but went on to tell me
how his own life as an alcoholic had been filled with such
blunders, and tragedy as well. When he finished, I agreed to go
with him on Saturday to get help.

By Friday night, though, I had decided not to go. As I sat
down for a typical evening of bourbon and TV, I began to watch
the film *Days of Wine and Roses,* the story of a marriage between
alcoholics, played by Jack Lemmon and Lee Remick. In one

scene, Jack Klugman, who plays a recovering alcoholic, told Lemmon what would happen if he kept drinking. Klugman slammed his fist on a table and yelled, "Nothing will have any meaning for you anymore—nothing, NOTHING!"

At that point I had a terrible flashback of when, in a drunken rage, a friend had picked up her beloved puppy and hurled him across the room. I looked at my cat. I became afraid that I might even hurt Mousse. I knew then I had to accept my neighbor's offer.

I did, and by the grace of God I've been sober for twelve years. Not long ago I watched that film again, and I waited for the all-important scene between Klugman and Lemmon. This time, though, there was just a conversation, one man explaining alcoholic progression to another. No banging on tables, no one shouting, "Nothing will have any meaning for you anymore." The words that changed my life had never been spoken.

 ## HER MOTHER'S VOICE
Lois Bunker Woods

The year is 1939. The place is an eighty-acre dairy farm outside the small town of Chehalis, Washington, sixteen miles from the nearest doctor or hospital. A little girl, an eighteen-month-old toddler dressed in overalls, slams the screen door as she ambles out onto the back porch to play in the sunshine. Her mother is inside the house, cleaning.

Outdoors on this warm spring morning the world is full of delights to explore. The youngster runs through the dewy grass, picks dandelions, and carries them back to the house. On the porch an old enameled kettle sitting in the sun catches her eye. It is filled with peas soaking in an arsenic solution, something that will prevent them from rotting when planted. Back then, seeds weren't pretreated as most are today.

The little girl is fascinated with the liquid in the kettle. Taking a battered tin cup, she dips it in the pot, fills it with the liquid, then lifts it.

Just then her mother hears a voice calling her, "Ella, Ella, come quick!" She follows the voice through the house and out the back door where she spots the little girl, the cup at her lips. Frantic, she grabs the toddler and empties the cup. She wipes the little girl's lips, but, no, the youngster hasn't had a drop of the poison. The mother arrived just in time.

I know this story well because I was that little girl, and the woman who rescued me was my mother. And as for the voice, Mother recognized it right away. It belonged to her mother, my grandmother. The mystery? My grandmother had died the year before, six months after I was born.

THE SEA ON MY BACK
George Plume

Every submariner lives with one terrifying fear: in a life-or-death situation he might have to shut the hatch or close a watertight door on shipmates, thus abandoning them to death—or even suffer the same fate himself. It is something you accept and never think about.

Certainly I wasn't thinking about it as the submarine USS *Harder* surged smoothly through that night in 1944. It was a routine evening on war patrol.

Yet, after almost twenty years I can still see that night, hear it, feel it . . . even smell it.

It was the night I *knew* there was a God—the night I experienced His real *power* and felt the indescribable wonder of His presence.

We were slipping along at ten knots, using the hours of darkness to recharge our batteries and air banks while patrolling on the surface. Lieutenant Sam Logan, a lanky whiz of a submarine officer, was the Officer of the Day on the bridge. The second section had relieved the watch at 2000 hours (8:00 P.M.) and I had taken over as quartermaster on watch.

The lookouts changed at staggered intervals, to prevent clogging the hatchway in the event the bridge watch had to come scrambling down. There was a man coming and going every half hour. Up through the control room hatch, turn, two steps over to the bridge ladder and up, using the dogwheel on the open hatch cover as a handle to pull themselves through the manhole.

On diving, the last man off deck yanks a lanyard that brings the cover slamming down. The quartermaster must then reach up and swiftly spin the dogwheel to extend the dog levers under the hatch rim into locking position.

Except for scattered rain squalls, visibility was good that night. With the enemy coast only an hour's flying time away, our lookouts were "keeping their binoculars warm."

I had just come back down into the conning tower after a topside look around when a low-flying Japanese patrol bomber burst out of a rain squall directly behind us, roaring in for the kill.

The after-lookout screamed the warning, "Clear the bridge!"

The three lookouts came tumbling down the hatch. As quartermaster on duty I leaped for the forward corner to be ready to help Logan secure the cover.

"Dive! Dive!" bellowed through the speakers. Down came Logan, lanyard in fist, pulling the hatchcover closed.

"He's right on top of us!" Logan panted.

Then he swiveled his head and shouted to the control room, "Take her deep . . . FAST!"

With the trip latch apparently engaged, Logan spun away to jump down the control room ladder and take over the dive. There wasn't *time* to wait for a "green board" signal below, which would signify all hull openings closed. Thirty seconds from the diving alarm our decks had plunged beneath the surface.

In those thirty seconds my surprise at the suddenness of the bomber attack turned to utter shock as water poured down upon me from the partially closed hatch. It was stuck and would not close.

I gripped the wheel desperately, twisting back and forth with all my strength, but it was immovable. Fighting water that all but blinded me, I looked over my left shoulder frantically. The helmsman had gone below, right behind Lt. Logan. I was alone.

There was a wild shout from below: "We still got a red light on the bridge hatch!"

But I couldn't answer. The descending water was a fierce torrent and I was choking as I kept up my maddened twisting and jerking at the dogwheel. Roaring in my ears, the terrible noise of the in-rushing sea increased.

A thunderous explosion sledgehammered the hull, then another, causing the *Harder* to jump convulsively. The submarine lurched sideways under the smashing blow of a third Japanese depth charge.

Then, over all the terrifying noise, I heard a heavy clang as the control room hatch slammed shut below. They had abandoned me!

Surfacing, to stop the uncontrollable flooding and save me, meant destruction for the *Harder* and death for every man on board. But I didn't think of that. I didn't think of anything. I tried to scream for help. And then I went berserk as I wrenched and tore at that jammed dogwheel. All *I* knew was that I didn't want to die—not alone in here—like this. The awful force above tore me away from the hatch mechanism, while inexorably from below, the water rose in that tiny, steel cubicle. I grabbed for the ladder . . .

I was paralyzed by fear beyond description, a miserable fright born of complete helplessness. Yet, deep within me was the recurring thought *God help me, God help me.* It was not an uttered or conscious prayer. My panic had carried me past such intelligence. I couldn't fight, I couldn't think. I couldn't *ask* for God's intervention.

And that is when it happened.

Suddenly, through the chaos, there came a quieting and a strange feeling of reassurance. It seemed, inexplicably, that in the few moments I had left there was plenty of time. Then from the calm within me came these words, which I shall hear for the rest of my days: "George, *open the hatch!*"

Without question or thought, obediently, and with strength that had left my body, I reached up. This time I turned the dogwheel *back,* to open the hatch. The dogs stuck for a heartbeat then slid back, easily . . . and the monstrous sea pressure immediately pressed the hatch tight on the rim! Instantly the crushing downpour dwindled to a trickle.

Methodically, I slowly reversed the wheel and secured the hatch. The trickle stopped. I turned to look about me in wonder. Then I forged through the water to get my hand on the speaker "talk" lever and said, "It's okay. The hatch is closed. You can pump this place out now."

I've marveled for years, in thinking back, that even then, without conscious thought I did *not* say, "I closed the hatch." The truth bespoke itself. The hatch *was* closed, but not by me.

The conning tower was pumped out, the hatch below opened, and I climbed down to rejoin my back-pounding, joyful shipmates. Commander Sam Dealey, one of the finest men I shall ever know, had quiet words of commendation as the boat cruised safely in the depths.

But through all of it there was that one question . . . that single, small, lingering doubt. I turned to Lt. Logan and asked, "Did anybody down here use the speaker to tell me to open the hatch?" The looks of surprise around the control room told me what I guess I already knew. Someone else had helped me.

Today, almost twenty years later, I still feel the mighty power of that reassurance—that He is a practical, ever-present God, that He has a plan for each of us. And in that knowledge I have a serene, indestructible, immovable faith that I, simply, humbly, and gratefully, try to share with those about me.

I'M GOING TO CRASH
Jack Armstrong

Things weren't going as I had expected that blustery March night in 1972 over Arkansas.

I was flying a single-engine four-seat Cherokee 180 from Chicago for delivery to Houston and had planned to reach Shreveport, Louisiana, that night. But as I passed over Fort Smith, Arkansas, I recomputed my ground speed and found that I was pushing into a head wind of much greater velocity than had been forecast. That meant I would not have enough fuel to reach Shreveport.

It was 8:00 P.M. A light rain beat against my windshield like scatter shot and a heavy overcast blocked out any moonlight. Even at my assigned altitude of seven thousand feet, I couldn't see a thing; it was pitch black outside my cockpit windows. Instrument weather.

No problem, though. Over my radio I requested clearance to land at nearby Texarkana, Arkansas.

Texarkana approach control came on clear: "Okay, Cherokee seven-nine-four-eight-n, descend and maintain two thousand feet; you are cleared for an instrument approach to the airport."

I settled back. I enjoyed these flights. Ever since I got out of the Navy in 1971, flying had been my main goal in life. And I was doing all right with it. I figured I could take care of myself.

I finished my landing check list and, by instrument check, found my position to be about thirty miles north-northwest of the Texarkana airport. I knew that a thick forest of pine trees and rolling hills were beneath me.

Suddenly my engine coughed, quit . . . started . . . and quit again! What was wrong? Frantically I checked instruments. There was plenty of fuel. I pushed controls, checked again. Nothing. A cold fear seized me.

Now only wind noise filled the cockpit as my 2450-pound plane began its inexorable drop to earth. I sat helpless at the dead controls as my ship hurtled into the total blackness. Terror shot through me as I thought of smashing into the thick pines that would tear my ship to shreds.

I began a series of emergency measures. I radioed a Mayday distress call to the air controller, advising him of my situation. Then I set the Cherokee into a glide speed of eighty miles an hour, extended-ten degree flaps, and noted that we were dropping 1100 feet per minute. That meant less than two minutes before we would crash. I still could not see anything outside the windows.

I then did the only other thing I could do. "O Lord Jesus," I prayed, "into Your hands I come."

Suddenly, unbelievably, a complete peace filled the cabin. Fear left me. In its place I felt a strange presence. Words seemed to fill my mind—words of calm and reassurance. *Everything is going to be all right. Look off your left wing.*

Then, through a clear spot in the murky skies, I saw a light from a house porch. Instinctively I swung the plane toward it.

Again the Voice in my mind. *Now look below to your right.*

When I looked, I saw the headlights of two cars coming toward me.

Head directly for those two cars; everything is going to be all right.

The deep indescribable feeling of peace and beauty intensified.

I kept heading toward the headlights; they were the only thing I could see outside the cockpit. The plane shuddered from wind gusts as we silently sped downward. I switched on my landing lights and continued on.

Whoosh! I passed about thirty feet over the first car and was immediately engulfed by tall dark trees racing close by on both sides. I sensed I was lined up with the highway, but I seemed to be flying into a tunnel.

The Voice kept assuring me. *Everything will be all right.*

Now the second car was facing me head-on and I felt sure we'd collide. I tried to turn the plane, but my hands and legs would not respond.

Keep heading for that car, continued the soft, soothing Voice. *Everything is going to be all right.*

My air speed had dropped drastically; the red stall light was frantically indicating that there wasn't enough air flow over my wings to maintain a safe glide.

Then I felt an impulse to do the strangest thing. Despite my critically low air speed, I was suddenly prompted to pull back on the controls, raising the plane's nose into a high attitude so that the lighter tail section would hit the oncoming car first. Ordinarily such a maneuver would lead to a total stall and crash. I waited for the impact.

There was none. Instead, the highway pavement appeared in my landing lights, rising steeply. I was heading uphill! But because of my high nose attitude, the plane set down on the concrete in a perfect three-point landing. I rolled to the top of the hill and began using my brakes. There at the side of the highway was a roadside café, its neon sign saying "Penney's Cafe" glowing. I kept using the brakes, rolled into the café's parking lot and stopped.

Suddenly the immensity of the incredible thing that had happened overwhelmed me. All I could do was sit there thanking God.

Light flooded the parking lot as the café door opened and a man walked toward me. "How did you get *here?*" he asked in astonishment.

"A miracle of God," I said in a choked voice.

I asked the man to check down the road; I was worried about

the people I might have run off the highway. After ten minutes he came back. He had found no one and did not recall seeing any cars earlier.

Were those lights real, I wondered, or had the Lord put them there just for me? All I know is that if I had not lifted my plane's nose to avoid the second car, I certainly would have slammed into the inclined highway. My lights did not shine far enough for me to react to landing uphill. The impact probably would have caused the plane to explode, since I had about fifteen gallons of fuel left in the wing tanks.

There was not a scratch on the plane. The air traffic controllers in Texarkana were amazed to find me alive. What had caused the engine to quit? A clogged fuel line.

I learned that the road I had landed on was U.S. Highway 71. So that night after I checked into a motel, just out of curiosity I picked up the Bible in my room and turned to the 71st psalm. It began, "In thee, O Lord, do I put my trust. Let me never be put to confusion. . . ."

I put the book down and looked out the window. The dark mist was falling and the sky was still black. But I knew that above that overcast sky the stars were still shining, though I couldn't see them. And now I knew, more certainly than ever before, that the Lord of Heaven was there as well.

I HEARD HIS CRIES
Virginia Ann Van Seters

I'm a sound sleeper. Only thirst or a headache ever wakes me up. A car speeding past, a dog barking, a passing thunderstorm—I can sleep through almost anything. But for no apparent reason I woke up with a start one cool fall night.

At first I thought it was time to get up. No, my clock showed 1:00 A.M. I listened. All was still, yet I felt as though I had awaked for some reason. I sat on the side of the bed, bolt upright. Several minutes passed. The bedroom windows were closed and the curtains drawn. No noise from the outside. There was total silence.

Then I heard, distinctly, a man's voice: "Help me, help me. Oh, please, help me!"

The voice sounded like it was in the room with me. "Help me, help me! Oh, please, help me!"

Immediately I called the police emergency number. "Someone needs help," I said, "out near my street." I told the dispatcher where I lived and, satisfied that I had done all I could, I went back to bed.

Even before I fell asleep, the police dispatcher called me back. She sounded incredulous. "How did you know someone was there?" she asked.

"I heard his cries," I said.

"But how could you?" she asked. She knew my condominium was set well back from the street. My windows were closed and I hadn't heard the police drive by. "The man you heard," she explained, "was trapped in a car at the bottom of a ravine nearly two blocks away."

"I heard him," I said. Somehow I heard him.

❄ UNSCHEDULED APPOINTMENT
Jeanne Murray Hill, R.N.

My flight home from a brief trip to New York had been a pleasant one—up until the last half-hour. Then, for no reason at all, apprehension began to gather in me like the dark clouds of the turbulence we'd just passed through over Texas.

But the turbulence hadn't unnerved me. After fifteen years of being a nurse, it takes a lot to rattle me. That's what was so strange about my unease. When the pilot announced, "We passed through the turbulence easily with only a small time loss," my hand shook so that I spilled my coffee. One thought flashed through my mind like a danger signal: *We'll be late landing in Phoenix.*

Why worry? I asked myself. I wasn't trying to make plane connections. I was just going home. My husband and children would be in no hurry. It had long been a practice in our family to make meeting planes a family-fun occasion. The children enjoyed watching the other planes land before the special plane was met. Then we would always have Cokes together in the airport before going home. So, there was no *reason* to be upset over being a few minutes late, I chided myself. That thought was followed by the warning, *Hurry!*

I looked about me. Who had spoken? Or had I only *felt* someone had spoken? In spite of my protesting logic I folded my blanket and returned it to the rack above the seat. Then I straightened myself and collected all my belongings as if we were on the ground, ready to disembark.

I felt no calmer once my things were collected. In fact, I felt more upset. I glanced at my watch. How ridiculous! Fifteen more minutes. I asked the stewardess for a glass of water and fumbled in my purse for an air-sickness pill. But, as I fingered the white capsule, again I felt it. *No. The pill will relax you. And you will need to hurry!*

But why would I need to hurry? I'd just phoned my family before getting on the plane. They were all well and safe— unless they had had an accident on the way to the airport. No, I was sure that my family was all right. But I didn't take the pill.

For the next fifteen minutes I sat, belongings in hand, waiting to land. Soon below us Phoenix was a glistening canopy of lights in the black night.

"When will we land?" the man behind me asked the stewardess. "Are we very late?"

"Any minute now," she answered, checking her watch. "We'll be about four minutes late." Her words sent a chill through me. *You should be down there now!* But what possible difference could four minutes make?

Yet, I felt it again. *Hurry up. Get out your baggage stubs.* The words were felt more than actually heard, so definite this time that I obeyed without question. The plane landed safely and taxied to the terminal.

When the "fasten your seat belts" sign flashed off, I jumped out of my seat and scrambled down the ramp. I was glad to see my family well and safe. But still that didn't relieve my feeling of anxiety. A stronger force was now guiding my very footsteps. I barely kissed the family, scooped up my four-year-old into my arms, and kept walking. My husband glanced at me questioningly when I headed away from the restaurant, the scene of our usual gab-fest.

"I *need* to get my baggage," I called over the children's heads. They followed me reluctantly toward the baggage depot. There I could see my two blue suitcases, but something else caught my eye!

Three feet in front of my bags was a small cluster of people around a wheelchair. *Hurry up! Go to him! You're late!* I ran to the group and pushed my way through. A man in his sixties lay slumped in the chair. His skin was ashen. "He's got a chronic lung condition, but he's never been this bad before," said the man's wife, her voice shaking.

"I'm a nurse," I said. I examined the man. He wasn't breathing. There was no pulse. I put my ear to his chest; I thought I heard a very faint heartbeat.

"Dear God, help me," I said under my breath, then aloud: "You! Call an ambulance," I pointed to a young man in the tiny gathering. To another I said, "Call the Fire Rescue Squad."

"Louis," I turned to my husband, "help me get him to the floor."

Once the ill man was flat on the floor, I began mouth-to-mouth resuscitation, alternately blowing, resting, not daring to stop. By the time another nurse, also a passenger, arrived on the scene, an occasional beat of the man's heart could be felt in the pulse at his wrist.

The additional nurse and I were able to massage the heart externally. We continued mouth-to-mouth resuscitation until the Fire Rescue Squad came with an oxygen unit. Then a passing doctor arrived to help us. By now, the ill man's pulse was becoming more and more frequent.

When the ambulance arrived ten minutes later, his color had changed from ashen to life-pink.

My children, who had stayed off to the side, out of the way, joined my husband and me as we watched the ambulance drive off.

"I've got your suitcases, Mom," my son said.

"Thanks," I murmured, and then I said another heartfelt "thanks" to that voice I'd felt—to the One who knew that four minutes made the difference between life and death.

A phone call to the hospital the next day reassured me that the man would fully recover. I've recovered too—recovered my faith that over the years had become so casual I no longer expected the type of guidance that came to me on the airplane.

Yet, I know now that God can speak to us in many ways. He can even nudge us to hurry when He has a job for us.

❄ THE VOICE I DIDN'T WANT TO
❄ HEAR
Ingrid Widdell

Whenever I hear people debating whether God really contacts people with specific instructions, my mind goes back to an episode in my own life several years ago. It started in church one Saturday evening in my hometown of Gothenburg (Göteborg), Sweden, a persistent thought that had nothing to do with the service or the sermon but would not let me alone.

Go down to the harbor!

The harbor? At night? Me, a lone woman, go down to the roughest part of town? I impatiently thrust away the idea.

But it would not go. As distinctly as though a voice were pronouncing it I heard again, *I want you to go down to the harbor.*

Suppose it was a message from God Himself? But why would He send me to such a place on a dark and windy October night? I pictured the wet railroad tracks along the wharves, the deserted sheds and huge lonely cranes, the drunks and the prostitutes who roamed the area. And I turned my mind firmly back to the sermon.

It was no good, I couldn't concentrate. Each time the minister paused, that other thought was waiting for me.

"I have work for you to do at the harbor."

I squirmed in my pew until the service ended, then hurried home as fast as I could to put as much distance as possible between myself and this alarming idea. I actually slammed my door when I got inside, and at last the mysterious voice was silent.

But not my conscience. The event had a sort of sharp edge to it. As weeks went by, I could still recall the reality and clarity of that command, and I became more and more convinced that it had, in fact, come from God Himself.

And then suddenly one evening toward the end of November, the voice was back. *Go down to the harbor tonight.*

Near me lived an elderly couple who were members of my church and who, I knew, had had several experiences of divine guidance. Now I went to their house and told them the amazing instruction I seemed to be getting. They seemed to find it neither surprising nor particularly unusual.

"I'm an old fellow," the husband said, "and not much protection, but I'll come along with you anyway." And so the two of us set out.

The harbor in Gothenburg is big and that night there were many vessels in port. Where in all this area were we supposed to go?

We asked God to tell us and right away we had the distinct impression that we were to go on board a freighter.

But what one? Which dock?

The answer we seemed to receive was that we should try boarding the first vessel we came to. If we were refused, this was the wrong one. Eventually we would come to a ship we could walk straight on.

First at the pier before us was a big tanker. A watchman at the gangway looked so formidable that we did not even approach him. When we boarded the next two vessels, watchmen quickly accosted us and asked our business. Twice I opened my mouth to explain about the voice; twice I closed it and backed meekly down the gangplank. Soon we were standing in front of a Scottish freighter, which appeared to be deserted. Still, in obedience to our instructions, we went aboard. On the deck we saw a tiny beam of light coming from beneath a door. Opening it, we found ourselves at the head of a stairway up which came the sound of noisy voices. We went down.

And stepped straight into a wardroom filled with crewmen in all degrees of intoxication. "Welcome!" several thickly cordial voices greeted us. One of the men gallantly swept some bottles aside to make more room at the table. "Sit down! Have a drink!"

We accepted the seat but found declining the drink in our clumsy English a little more difficult. Soon an awkward silence fell over the room. At last there was nothing to do but to blurt out something about docks and voices and a job that maybe God wanted me to do.

Soon I found myself talking as rapidly about God as my English permitted, and how I had found a new life when I turned to Him for forgiveness some years ago.

A sound behind me made me turn. In the doorway stood a tall middle-aged man with a week's growth of beard on his chin, an empty bottle in one hand, and the filthiest suit of clothes I'd ever seen.

"Ian . . ." someone muttered. "Come in and sit down." Ian swayed in and stopped in front of me. Evidently he had been listening for some time for he burst out: "She's right, she's right. Don't you think I know . . . but that was long ago . . . ten dirty black years have gone since I ran away from God."

He leaned against the table as he spoke. Nobody said a word. He told about the church he had attended, about his wife, his children, and how he had lost them when he started to drink. Then something seemed to flash through his brain. He pointed the bottle at me and shouted:

"I'm that job, Miss! I'm the one God sent you to find!"

My heart was thumping. What on earth should I do now? The room was silent as the men seemed to ponder all this.

I started to pray silently and then I heard myself saying, "On Saturday nights we have a service at our church. Will you come with me, Ian? I will pick you up at eight o'clock."

"I'll be ready," he said.

A few minutes later we said goodbye to the sailors and left.

The rest of the week doubt fought with the hope building in me. The man had probably forgotten the whole thing by the next morning! But on Saturday night my old friend and I were back at the dock. The Scottish vessel was still there. My heart leaped when Ian came down the gangplank nicely dressed in hat and overcoat—and sober.

That night Ian sat beside me while I whispered translations of the Swedish service to him. At the close, when several people went into another room for prayer, I asked Ian if he, too, wanted to go. He nodded a silent yes.

We knelt with the others and here this modern prodigal son experienced his Heavenly Father's forgiveness. When Ian stood up, you could almost see the inner light radiating from him and you could sense his new peace of soul.

Five weeks later I was back at the harbor to meet the Scottish freighter when it anchored. Looking tanned and clear-eyed, Ian greeted me. He told me he had gone back to his family and asked them to forgive him. "The hardest thing was to face my children. But with God's grace I'll be a father to them yet."

As for his wife, he said, "She told me that never once in all those years did she stop praying for me."

Then I knew how God had answered those prayers. He had followed Ian's ship across the North Sea to give a lost soul another chance. And He had given me a second chance as well. That windy night in October when I first heard and failed to obey that voice, that was the night Ian's ship had first docked in Gothenburg.

GOD

Increases

STRENGTH

He gives power to the faint,
and to him who has no might he increases strength.
. . . .
they who wait for the Lord shall renew their strength,
they shall mount up with wings like eagles,
they shall run and not be weary,
they shall walk and not faint.

—ISAIAH 40:29–31, RSV

HE GIVETH MORE GRACE
—Annie Johnson Flint

He giveth more grace when the burdens grow greater,
    He sendeth more strength when the labors increase;
To added affliction He addeth His mercy,
    To multiplied trials, His multiplied peace.

When we have exhausted our store of endurance,
    When our strength has failed ere the day is half done,
When we reach the end of our hoarded resources,
    Our Father's full giving is only begun.

His love has no limit, his grace has no measure
    His power has no boundaries known unto men;
For out of his infinite riches in Jesus
    He giveth and giveth and giveth again.

MAMA, COME QUICK
Joan B. Paris

After my grandfather died, my uncle Bill was the only one left living in the old family home with my grandmother. She was ninety-three and he was sixty-five, but they depended on each other like siblings. He'd get the Nashville newspaper every morning and bring her breakfast and keep her up-to-date on the rest of the family.

One morning, though, after twenty-three years of the same routine, he got up at seven o'clock, swung both feet over the side of his bed, and suddenly collapsed to the floor with a stroke. Conscious but unable to move, he yelled to my grandmother in her bedroom, "Mama, Mama!"

"Why are you hollering so early in the morning?" she called back, roused from her sleep.

"Mama," he said, "come quick."

Grandmother knew then that something was terribly wrong. Quickly she called to the One who had never failed to hear her every prayer, then got out of bed. She hurried to my uncle's room, where he lay paralyzed. Knowing help was needed, she telephoned their next-door neighbor and went downstairs to let the neighbor in. Together they went to Bill's room; medical help was summoned and soon arrived.

What was so unusual about this? Wouldn't any mother have done the same? Yes, perhaps. But you see, Grandmother had been permanently injured in a car accident and since then had fallen, breaking her hip twice. She had been in a wheelchair for nine years. During that time she had not taken one step by herself.

SEND SOMEONE . . . ANYONE!
Mildred Shell, as told to Jorunn O. Ricketts

On that sunny August afternoon several years ago, there was no indication that anything could mar the beauty and peace of the day. It was a Friday, and I could hear the hum of my husband's tractor as he mowed the grass in the field next to our backyard.

Our house stands on a hill above the highway about a mile from the little town of Marble Hill, Missouri. Mr. Stephens, a farmer, is our nearest neighbor and he lives a quarter of a mile down the road.

I don't know what it was that caused me to turn suddenly and look at my husband on the tractor. As I did so, I watched in horror and disbelief as the tractor hit something hard in the grass, then turned over, pinning my husband beneath.

In a panic I began running toward the tractor knowing that I had to get Howard out from under before it burst into flames.

Jack, our ten-year-old son, was already by his father's side. Together we pulled and pried, but all our efforts seemed only to hurt Howard, who was lying on his back with the steering wheel pressing against his chest. One of his legs was caught under the back end of the heavy machine, a Farmall Cut, which weighed three thousand pounds.

Our cries for help rang out across the empty field. We could hear the cars go by on the highway, but they couldn't possibly hear us.

Howard was struggling to breathe—if the weight of the tractor wasn't lifted off his chest, he might die! Frantically we searched for something to prop up the tractor. There was nothing.

O God, I thought in despair, *send someone . . . anyone!*

I didn't stop to think how hopelessly ridiculous it would be for a woman alone to try to lift a tractor. I only knew that Howard would die if it wasn't done. With one shoulder leaning against the radiator, I took hold and lifted with all my might . . . and the tractor moved. I was holding it up, thank God! Howard was breathing easier. He was saved, at least for the moment.

"You try and pull Daddy out," I said to Jack. "I'll hold the tractor."

Jack was pulling as hard as he could, but Howard wasn't moving.

"I can't." Howard was straining to breathe and talk at the same time. "A rock . . . under my back . . . I'm hurt." His leg was still pinned under the tractor. It was obvious that we couldn't get him out without help.

"Run," I said to Jack. "Phone Mr. Stephens and ask him to bring help."

I watched Jack race across the yard and into the house and prayed that our neighbor was at home.

Then, for a while, it was as if time had been suspended. I didn't seem to be aware of the weight of the tractor and I wasn't even bothered by the heat. Meanwhile, Howard was struggling to speak. "I . . . can't . . . take . . . it . . . much . . . longer."

In many private conversations Howard and I had agreed that death was not something to fear. We had surrendered our lives to God many years before. Miraculously, we felt, He had brought Howard back after a head wound nearly killed him on Saipan during World War II. And now, once again, Howard was in God's hands. With a sudden calmness I knew that if Howard was to live, God would use me to hold up the tractor till help came.

Finally I saw them running toward us—Jack and Mr. Stephens and his son, Jerry, and Henry Thiele, another neighbor. Together they lifted the tractor. The doctor arrived, and then the ambulance. Howard's leg had to be stitched up, and the doctor said X rays would be necessary. "But I don't think he's seriously hurt."

Then Mr. Stephens took my right arm firmly and said, "Now I'll take *you* to the doctor."

"Me, what in the world for?" I could feel no pain anywhere. But then I looked and saw that the skin and flesh of my left arm and shoulder was hanging in shreds. I could hardly believe what I saw. At the clinic the doctor explained that the heat from the radiator had actually cooked the flesh on my arm and shoulder to the bone.

In a few days Howard came home in a wheelchair to nurse a crushed vertebra in his back. My left arm was helpless until the burnt muscles slowly healed. For months we were quite a pair, both semi-invalids with a house and two children to care for.

Every time we think back to that August Friday, we marvel at the way things worked out. When Jack telephoned our neighbor for help, Mr. Stephens just *happened* to walk into his kitchen in time to take the call. His son Jerry, who no longer lives at home, just *happened* to be there visiting that day.

And all the while God was lifting that tractor for almost one hour. I wasn't. On my own I couldn't. We still have the tractor, and I have since tried lifting the front end. I can't budge it.

 ## CROSSINGS
—Lee Webber

I came to the swift, raging river,
 And the roar held the echo of fear;
"Oh, Lord, give me wings to fly over,
 If You are, as You promised, quite near."

But He said, "Trust the grace I am giving,
 All-pervasive, sufficient for you.
Take My hand—we will face this together;
 But My plan is—not over, but through."

THEY SAY—I RISKED MY LIFE
Harold D. Walters

"If you go through with it, Walters, it may cost you your life," the doctor warned me.

I sat there numbly, slumped down in his office chair. Idly, I picked at the loose thread on my coat button. The words had sunk into my subconscious mind, but as yet I hadn't fully translated them.

"You should go to bed at once to prevent any more hemorrhages. In the very near future we will get you off to a dry climate," the doctor continued. "Can't take chances with tuberculosis."

I got up, put on my top coat, and carefully smoothed out a wrinkle in my hat. I avoided looking again at the sympathy I knew would be in the doctor's face. The air in his office seemed unbearably close and hot.

Outside I paused a moment and looked toward the street. The late afternoon shadow cut directly down the middle of my car, leaving one half a bright orange and the other a drab brown.

"Good afternoon, Mr. Walters." The voice—that of a woman on the sidewalk—came from a thousand miles away. "We're looking forward so much to the performance tomorrow. My two sisters drove all the way from Des Moines to see you play the Christus."

Her words thumped dully against my eardrums. I walked by her to my car, reaching for my key case. Traffic was heavier than usual. People even now were arriving from hundreds of miles away for the final performance of the Passion Play tomorrow. The Scottish Rite Temple Auditorium here in Bloomington, Illinois, would bulge with fifteen hundred of them.

"No it won't," I said, half to myself, half out loud. I had a crazy desire to go out into the street, stop traffic, and tell 'em all to go back home. *Because there wasn't going to be a Passion Play tomorrow.*

Back at home in my study chair, I began to think more coherently. Perhaps it wasn't the end of everything. A few months in New Mexico . . . maybe a year . . . a gradual return to normal health . . . then here again to my insurance business—and the Passion Play. Some of the mist began to clear away.

I made an effort to rise and phone Delmar Darrah, director of the play. Better tell him now and get it over with. But a heavy weight in my chest held me down. Who would he get to understudy? I alone could play Jesus tomorrow. The play would have to be called off.

Bitterness welled up inside me. Why this to me? Had God decided suddenly that I was unworthy to play the role of Jesus?

Then, like a white light ripping into a dark room, came a new thought. *I have lived many glorious hours as Christ, if only in a play.* I had poured my whole being into the part—had tried to think and act like He would. *Right now, in this very room, I will try to be as He would be.* What would Jesus do in my situation? I sat deep in thought for a long time.

Later I arose from the chair, moved over to the telephone, and dialed a number. "Doctor," I said, "I will follow your instructions to the letter—after I do the final presentation tomorrow."

I explained to my family that I was not trying to be melodramatic or heroic and was happy when they agreed even though they were fearful. After quiet meditation the solution had seemed so very simple. The Passion Play was an inspiring, holy masterpiece. Tomorrow it would uplift some fifteen hundred people. It would bring God a little closer to every one of them. This seemed to more than justify any physical danger chanced by one unimportant human being.

The next day I arrived at the auditorium in plenty of time to do a slow careful job on my makeup. I didn't want to be hurried or rushed. Every bit of strength had to be saved for the performance itself.

As I sat in the dressing room, fingering the familiar makeup boxes and sniffing the pungent odor of grease paint, I thought how much I had loved playing this role. This 1940 performance would be my third since I had earned the part in 1938. Many thoughts darted through my head. I suppose it is normal for one who plays the Christus to want to try, regardless of how inadequately, to pattern his life after the Prince of Peace. I had spent much of my time teaching Sunday school and preaching sermons to help spread the gospel. In the Passion Play I had found a way to bring a message to thousands of people far more effectively than from a pulpit. I loved these hours more than anything else in life.

Then I had a sudden spasm in my chest—worse than any before.

The man helping me with my makeup was aghast. Quickly he helped me over to a couch. Then he started to bolt for the door—to tell the others.

I grabbed his coat. "Please?" I shook my head weakly. "I'll be all right in a minute."

"You'll kill yourself!" he protested. But I made him promise not to say anything.

When strength returned, I resumed my makeup. Curtain time was at hand. During final adjustments to my costume I thankfully noted that the dark beard and paint almost completely concealed my pale features.

Before leaving the dressing room, I lowered my head for a moment. "Please, Lord, am I doing Your will, or is it just pride that is driving me on? Let me do what is right." I knew that only with His help and strength would I be able to go through with the performance. I was confident that He would not fail me.

The play opened on schedule at 1:30 P.M. The curtains parted, the light shone from above, and I, as Jesus, was in the opening scene giving the Sermon on the Mount.

At the end of the first scene I was exhausted. Moving about and talking had been torture. The salt taste of blood was in my mouth from internal bleeding.

During the second-scene curtain I had to lie down for a moment. "What's wrong with Walters?" I heard someone ask. "Temperament," a stagehand replied significantly.

I smiled wryly to myself. But at that moment all that mattered to me was whether I could finish. The words of Jesus on the cross never had such sharp meaning—"My God, my God, why hast thou forsaken me?"

In this moment of near collapse I remembered, like a message, a casually made statement by one of the actors who in real life is a linotype operator for Bloomington's only newspaper. "Once a year," he had said, "I have a chance to be John the Disciple, not just Clifton Webb of Bloomington. And for those hours *I am* Disciple John."

Here was my answer. I could not be Harold Walters and ever go through with the rest of the play. I had to forget myself, my pain, my fears, everything *but being Jesus . . .*

Back on the stage I began to lose myself in Him. The tremendous beauty and excitement of the role swept me up. The pain left my chest. My voice grew stronger—clearer. Strength poured into my arms and legs. The moments became sheer splendor. I wanted them to last forever.

When the final curtain went down, I glowed with exhilaration. God had come. He had poured His strength into me. For those sublime moments His divine Spirit had been in me.

When a rest cure of six months in New Mexico ended my illness, I returned to Bloomington at once. It was time to begin preparations for my role of Christus again.

Today I am considered to have an arrested case of tuberculosis. Two years ago I was able to buy more life insurance.

This April 4 (1948) I will play the role of Christus again for the eleventh straight year. Few moments of real bliss come to a man's life. But once each year I have them—during the Passion Play.

I also believe that some time in every person's life comes a real test of faith—some moment when it seems foolhardy, even wrong, to try to follow the Footsteps. I am convinced that no one can ever meet this test alone. It can only be done with the help of God, through prayer, and an uncompromising desire to do His will.

 ## THIN ICE
William G. Benkelman

The temperature had hovered between freezing and zero for almost a week. When I got home from work that Friday in February 1975, I glanced at the frozen Rocky River, just a few feet from our door—and it looked inviting.

"What about having some friends over for skating tonight?" I asked my wife, Sylva. Whenever the ice was good, we liked to floodlight the area behind our house and play skating music on the hi-fi. Afterward skaters would come upstairs for cookies and coffee before a roaring fire in our living room. But this time Sylva said no. She is a registered nurse and she had been working at the hospital since 7:00 A.M., so she was very tired.

The sun was still shining and I figured there would be a good half hour before dark for me to skate. Down the stairs I went and put on my skates on the dock under our house. The ice tested very strong, the temperature was twenty-two degrees, and there was no wind—a great combination. It was exhilarating. At a smooth clip I traveled across the lagoon in back of our house and suddenly felt so invigorated that I decided to skate on—to the river, up the west channel, and around the island on which the Cleveland Yachting Club is located. The club was closed for February; it looked like a ghost town of dry-docked boats.

"Great skating!" I shouted happily to a woman skating with some children, the only people around. I shot ahead, under the little bridge that connected the island to the far bank, on and on until I headed once more into the river, clipping along, now in the middle, a hundred feet from shore, when . . .

Oh, oh—a patch of soft ice. Slush. I thought I could coast through it, but I slowed down. I stroked with my right foot; the ice gave way under it. I tried to stroke with the other, but *it* broke through. I was in trouble. Bad trouble.

Immediately I knew why. It was because of the big bridge high above me. For days the city had been spreading salt on it to melt the snow on the roadbed. The salt had filtered down to the river, softening the wide path of ice I had skated into. Now I found myself sinking through the ice, then suddenly plunging up to my neck in freezing water.

I did not panic. I did not thrash about. I hollered. I pounded away at the mushy ice in an attempt to reach ice firm enough to support me. I knew I had to do something fast, for I had read somewhere that a person can survive only three minutes in freezing water. I was aware, too, of an unusual fact about myself—that I am incapable of floating. I'm so thin, more bones than flesh, that I have what is called negative buoyancy—when I'm not moving my arms or legs in water, I sink to the bottom.

I tried to work myself toward firmer ice by breaking off small pieces along the edge. But it was taking too much time. This way I'd freeze to death before I'd ever get out. I could hear no one answering my cries; the bridge above me was humming with rush-hour traffic, yet I knew, because of the railing and the angle, that no one in a passing car could see me. I simply had to think of another way to get myself out of the water.

Then it came to me. I swim regularly, every week, and it was not unusual for me to swim the length of the "Y" pool underwater. I looked at the shore a hundred feet away and realized that if I could swim that distance under the ice, I could break through at the shore. It was a gamble, but I saw no hope any other way. I took one last look around to see if anyone was in sight. No one. "And if I don't make it," I said to myself, "no one except God will ever know what happened."

There in the water, about to dive under the ice, thinking of God, I felt ashamed before Him. "I'm sorry," I prayed to Him. "I'm sorry I've been so careless with Your precious gift of life. I want to live, God. I want desperately to live, but I'll accept Your will."

In those brief moments I didn't ask God to save my life. It had been a long time since I had asked Him for anything at all. Sylva and I had married in 1953 and, of course, we wanted children. We did everything we could, including a lot of praying, but no children came. After praying for ten years I had come to the conclusion that God wasn't listening to me.

But He was listening now. I wasn't asking Him for help or for my life, yet now He was present; I could feel His closeness as I prepared myself for the plunge under the ice.

Don't do it! came the feeling.

I was mystified. I had set my mind on the plan.

Don't do it! came the feeling again.

My mind told me one thing, but His presence told me another. I had to decide now, this second.

I gave myself over to that inner command. But then I had no hope.

It was a matter of minutes, maybe two, when I saw the police car on the yachting club island and nearby, across the stretch of obviously treacherous ice, I saw a policeman standing in the dusk, looking at me. "Throw me a rope!" I yelled. He disappeared. At first I had had a surge of optimism, but now that he was gone from me, I despaired. "Hurry," I said to myself frantically. "Hurry!" Could he know how little time I had left?

I heard voices. "We're going to throw you a rope."

Throw it now! I thought to myself. I could feel the paralysis setting in. It came fast. At first I couldn't move my legs. My arms stiffened. There was no part of me that I could move. No longer now was I thinking about ropes. I was thinking about . . . boyhood vacations on Mackinac Island . . . Sylva and me on a flying honeymoon . . . sailing on a moonlit night . . .

My hands . . . I saw my hands slip away from the surface of the ice. Yet I was experiencing a peace that was serene and actually pleasant. I felt my head go under the water. I felt icy water entering my mouth. I was sinking, but now I could move neither arms nor legs. I was rigid.

And then, suddenly, mysteriously, the power was there. I *could* move my arms. I pushed them down in the water. My head came up. I breathed again. And there in front of me was an orange life preserver. The last thing I remember was reaching for it.

o   o   o

My next awareness was opening my eyes and seeing the doctor peering into my face. He said, "There's someone here I'm sure you want to see." It was Sylva.

"How did I get here?" I asked, bewildered. Her answer was a litany of many miracles.

A bus was crossing the bridge at the precise moment I fell through the ice. The driver, sitting high up, saw me and radioed his dispatcher, who called the police. A girl happened to be walking along our river-front road on her way to a baby-sitting job. She heard my cries for help and rushed to our neighbor's house. The neighbor stepped outside, saw me in the river, and then she also called the police.

A policeman came, then went to his car to radio for extra help, while I held on to the orange life preserver that had been thrown to me. My rescuers were able to walk about halfway out on the ice before it started to crack, and a rope was thrown, which they say I grabbed, but let slip through my hands when they started to pull on it.

By then a crowd had gathered on the island. Three times my head went under the water, each time the crowd gasping, shouting that I was gone, and three times my head came back up, spouting water. Finally a dinghy was found and one of the policemen rushed it to the spot where I was appearing and disappearing. I was submerged, completely out of sight before he could get to me, but he reached his arm down over the dinghy into the water and, miraculously, connected with the collar of my jacket. The dinghy nearly capsized as he tried to drag me into it, but he hung on to me as I dangled from its side, and we were pulled to safety. Oxygen in the ambulance kept me alive during the rush to the hospital.

Later I figured that I was in the freezing water a minimum of twelve minutes. I was unconscious for three hours. The doctor in the emergency room at the hospital said he never saw a person alive with a pH blood factor as low as mine—six. When I was in the icy water I was not aware of the pain, but I was shivering from cold when I came to, calling for blankets. I spent one night in the intensive-care unit of the hospital and, to the doctors' amazement, the patient who was in critical condition on arrival was permitted to return home the next day. Two months later my heart was back to normal, and eight months later the nerves in my arms and legs had regenerated.

It took about a week for me to believe fully that I wasn't just dreaming and was really living. Since then, life for me has taken on a new meaning. I am more appreciative of being alive. I feel very grateful to God for sparing my life and to the five people who had a major part in my rescue. Since then, too, a lot of questions have been answered for me.

Where did the message come from that stopped me from my rash plan to swim under the ice?

When my body was paralyzed, where did the power come from that let my arms move again?

When I was unconscious under the water, why didn't the current sweep me downstream?

I know the answers to those questions now, for I've learned that God is always listening. He hears our prayers. When it is within His plan to answer them, He can work miracles. He did for me.

GOD

Restores

HEALTH

For I will restore health to you,
and your wounds I will heal,

     says the LORD.

     —JEREMIAH 30:17, RSV

❄ WHEN I AM SORE BESET
—*Antoinette Goetschius*

When I am sore beset, I seek some quiet place,
Some lonely room or barren windswept hill,
And there in silence wait apart until
I see again the smile upon God's face,
Until His presence floods me like the dawn,
And I can hear His whispered, "Peace be still,"
And know again the strength to do His will.
I turn to take my load and find it gone.

❄ THE UNTOUCHABLE
Mark Miller

In June 1977, it seemed that everything was going my way. I'd
graduated from college with honors, had married Shirley, a
sweet, wonderful girl, and was working in my family's honey
business in southern California. I was planning to start law
school in September, and our first baby was due the same
month. How excited I felt. How fulfilled!

But early one morning that summer a frightening change
began to take place. I'd started out jogging my usual one-mile
circuit, and about halfway through it, the strength suddenly
went out of my body. I practically passed out. It was all I could
do to stagger back to the house and collapse on the couch.

What could be happening to me? My arms and legs felt as if
they were made of lead. I had no energy or vitality.

I went to a doctor who put me through a battery of tests. "It's
perplexing," he told me. "Your tests show nothing abnormal."
Doctor after doctor gave me the same answer.

Now, besides the extreme weakness and fatigue, I was gradually having nausea and other digestive troubles. I grew more
and more nervous and couldn't sleep. I entered a Loma Linda,
California, hospital for a thorough examination. Again, the

doctors found no abnormal test results. Yet something was terribly wrong with me.

We went on searching for a diagnosis. Shirley and I had been taught to take our problems to the Lord, and we prayed for some kind of reassurance. But it seemed that God wasn't answering. The doctors continued to be baffled.

In September I struggled to start law school, but soon, when I couldn't even muster the energy to walk to classes, I knew I had to give up. When our son Adam was born, I stood over his crib and prayed, "Please, Father, bless me with the strength to be a good father to this special little boy." How I longed for strength and guidance from my Father in Heaven! I felt lost, alone.

By the first of the year, 1978, it was clear that my condition was still worse. Gradually I began to notice the effect that certain ordinary things in the house had on me, things like cold cream or strong cleaning agents. A whiff of Shirley's perfume would make me feel dizzy and nauseated. On the day that our lawn was treated with chemical weed killer and fertilizer, I literally thought I was dying. I felt so much inner tension, so much pressure inside of me, it seemed my body would burst. We had to flee the house.

We went to my sister's. But as luck would have it, some workmen came to tar her roof. The fresh tar brought the same misery as the weed killer. We went to another relative's house until a road was resurfaced in the neighborhood, forcing us to leave. These common types of chemical application were toxic to me for an incredibly long time. We were driven to move at least a dozen times—to the homes of other relatives, to motels and apartments—all in an effort to find a place where I could just be sick without being violently ill.

During this period, morning and night, month after month, we went on praying. Family members and friends prayed for us consistently. Still, with all this outpouring of faith, my health didn't improve. And the months went by.

In January 1979, Shirley read about a hospital in Dallas with an Environmental Control Unit specializing in problems like mine. In February I was admitted to this unit at Brookhaven Medical Center, in the care of Dr. William Rea. For nearly six weeks, I underwent tests, many of them "double blind"—

which means that neither the nurse nor I knew whether I was being exposed to a chemical substance or pure water.

After Dr. Rea had analyzed the test results, he came to me. "You've had a breakdown in your immune system," he explained. "It's called 'environmental disease,' and it means you can't tolerate modern chemicals—none of them. The only cure we know is to avoid chemicals as much as possible—and hope your immune system gets enough rest to rebuild itself."

Just what this avoidance meant was brought home to us when a nurse gave me my instructions. "Drink only bottled water. All your food should come from farms where pesticides and other chemicals aren't used. Wear all-cotton clothing. Get rid of any synthetic furnishings in your house, and stay clear of chemical cleansers, detergents, and perfumes." She gave me a detailed list of things to avoid and information on how to go about it. Dr. Rea wished me well and urged me to stay in touch by telephone.

From that day on, my wife, Shirley, our son, Adam, and I became fugitives from twentieth-century chemicals. Back in California we found a two-family house in Santa Barbara near the ocean and began to live our lives according to the instructions I'd been given at the hospital. My condition seemed to improve, but only for a while. Five months after we'd left Brookhaven, our landlord, who lived above us, told me that exterminators were coming to spray for fleas. We left the house before the spraying and returned several hours later. Even with these precautions, the fumes were intolerable to me. I hurried away, while Shirley packed our things.

Again, we were on the run, living with different family members throughout California, Arizona, and Utah, never able to stay long in any one place. Our second son, Jarom, was born in March 1980, but I was not free to enjoy him. By now I was sleeping in my car in the hills at night to avoid the chemicals used in neighborhoods and farming areas. I came home to my family just long enough to eat a couple of times a day. In between, sick and weak, I sometimes sat in the car in a parking lot, praying, reading my Bible, feeling a kinship with Jesus—especially when I read His words to the scribe: "Foxes have holes, and birds of the air have nests; but the Son of man has nowhere to lay his head" (Matthew 8:20).

Sometimes I wrote in the journal I'd been keeping all my

adult life. This is the entry for May 3, 1980: "How horrible I feel! The people across the street put chemical fertilizers on their lawn. I stayed too long, and now I'm very sick. I feel like everything is hopeless. I want to die. Why must I suffer on and on and on? I feel like every cell in my body is going to burst. God, help me, please."

I continued to live in my car until August, when we decided to try moving into my parents' home in the Los Angeles area again. We told our neighbors about my problem, and they gladly cooperated by not using outdoor chemicals. But the months of running had weakened me further, and my basic intolerance was worse, especially my skin sensitivity. I had to be extremely careful of everything I touched or wore, and where I sat or lay down. The house had to be off limits to outsiders because of the chemical residues they would bring in. Whenever members of my own family returned from work or shopping, they had to shower and change into clothes worn only at home. I could only bear having the television on for a brief time because the plastic components gave off fumes when they heated up. My reading was limited to books that were old and out of public circulation; otherwise ink fumes and chemical residues affected me.

Dr. Rea offered suggestions and encouragement over the phone as best he could. Meanwhile, I'd found a doctor in nearby Malibu, Dr. Edward Wagner, who understood my condition and who was a great comfort to me because he was a spiritual man. It was about this time that I started rereading the Book of Job in the Bible. I was fascinated by this ancient story of an upright man undergoing troubles and torment that he had done nothing to deserve, marveling at the parallels I found with my own condition. I saw Job afflicted and living in constant pain, but steadfastly refusing to turn his back on God.

I had thought of suicide. Job had wanted to die, too. But he never lost faith in God: "Though he slay me, yet will I trust in him," Job said resolutely (13:15).

When my own pain and despair threatened to overwhelm me, I clung to that. Could I be like Job? Could I keep my faith, no matter what?

When my twenty-seventh birthday came, there was no earthly possession I wanted—or could use. Instead of gifts, I asked for a day of fasting and prayer. We knelt in a circle as a family and, one by one, prayed to our Heavenly Father. We thanked Him for the many things we had learned, and asked Him if He would please restore my health. We had a warm feeling in our hearts, knowing our prayers were heard. But in the days that followed, my skin became so sensitive that the slightest contact would burn like fire. Sometimes my reaction and tension were so severe that I'd gasp for breath, scream and cry, then fall to the rug, limp and exhausted.

It was so hard for my little boys to remember not to touch their daddy. One morning when I came out of my room while the rest of the family were having breakfast, Jarom tried to run to me.

"Daddy! Daddy!" he called, a delighted grin on his face, his arms reaching for me.

How I wanted to sweep him up in my arms, nuzzle his neck, and carry him for a piggyback ride around the table. But I had to turn away. It broke my heart.

Finally the day came when I asked Shirley to take the boys and move back to her parents' home in Utah. She had to do it, for the children's sakes as well as for my own physical health.

Saying good-bye, we cried. We knew we couldn't be together again as a family until my health improved. And I had never been worse!

Once more I went back to the Bible, back to the words of Job: "My lyre is turned to mourning, and my pipe to the voice of those who weep" (30:31, RSV). "Yes," I said out loud, "Job felt as I feel." Then I read on: "With God are wisdom and might; he has counsel and understanding" (12:13, RSV) and "When he has tried me, I shall come forth as gold" (23:10, RSV). "Yes," I said, "I must believe that. I must. I must."

My immunity weakened to the point where I had to stay in one room, isolated from everyone, never venturing into the rest of the house. I talked to my mother on the intercom. She cooked my meals and left my food on a tray outside the door. If she so much as picked up the tray after using a detergent on her hands, I would get a severe reaction if I touched that spot on the tray. My only contact with the outside world was the telephone, but even holding the plastic receiver too long could make me dizzy and anxious. I was a prisoner, an untouchable. I was desperately alone.

Then, during this time of extreme loneliness and despair, an

answer came to our four years of praying. I began to feel a deep
peace within me, a peace I had *never* felt before. I heard no
voices. I saw no angels. Yet I had a powerful conviction in my
heart and mind. Something in me seemed to say the words, *You
will be well very, very soon.*

I did not seem to improve, but the warmth and peace I felt
lasted for four weeks, during June and July 1981.

Then, on the morning of July 20, I was aware of a sense of
deep sorrow. I felt hopeless against some dark power greater
than my own. But, just as I thought I'd be completely overcome
with loneliness and sadness, it happened. I felt myself lifted on
eagles' wings; I seemed to soar beyond the fog and clouds into
the clear blue sky. A warmth suffused my whole body, a healing
warmth. The invisible bars fell away. I felt suddenly, totally,
confidently free. Free! With a new strength pouring into me, I
went to the bedroom door. Quietly I pushed it open, knowing
absolutely that I no longer needed to fear the outside world. My
eyes filled with tears. I found my mother and hugged her.

"Mark!" she whispered. "What's happened?"

"I'm well," I said firmly. "I've been healed." I *knew* it was so.

I couldn't wait to get back to Shirley and the children. I got
in our car only to find it wouldn't start. I tried to prime it by
putting gasoline in the carburetor, and I spilled some all over
my hand. But there was no toxic reaction. Nothing. "O God,
thank You. Thank You."

Within forty-eight hours I was on my way to Utah and my
family. Wanting to surprise them, I waited until I was a short
distance away and then telephoned.

"Hi, Shirley."

"Hello, sweetheart. How are you feeling today?"

"I'm better."

"I'm glad you're having a better day today."

"No, I'm well. I'm healed. I'm in Fillmore, and I'll be there
soon to bring you home."

Shirley could hardly find words. "Should we change our
clothes?" she finally asked. "Should we fix a special room for
you?"

"All of that's behind us. The Lord has made me well."

When I drove up to the house, Shirley, Adam, and Jarom
were waiting on the steps for me. No words can express the joy I
felt as I wrapped my arms around them. God had truly wrought

a glorious miracle in our lives. Later I went to Dallas and Dr. Rea examined me. He was thrilled by my unusual recovery. "You're totally tolerant and totally well," he told me.

Currently, I'm working in the family honey business, operating a honey store in the mountain apple-orchard community of Oak Glen, California. At church I enjoy teaching a Sunday school class.

At home, I love being a normal husband and daddy. My little boys can run to me whenever they want. And Shirley says, "I know how Lazarus' family must have felt when he walked out of the tomb."

I am alive again after four years of a living death. I give all the credit to our Father in Heaven, who loves us and hears us. I have learned that no matter how much we may have to suffer, we never have more than we can bear. I have learned that if you hang on to your faith, as Job did, God answers your prayers in His own perfect way.

THE MESSAGE
Ginger Davis Gettle

"I'm going to die, aren't I?" I said to my husband. "Tell me!"

Bob pulled his chair close to my hospital bed and took my hand. "You have to have another operation," he said, "maybe two. The tests taken after your stroke show you have two weak spots in the arteries in your brain. If they're not repaired, you'll have another stroke." He didn't add, ". . .and *that* stroke will be fatal," but I knew that's what he meant.

I pulled my hand away. "How much will it cost?"

His voice sank to a whisper. "About two hundred and fifty thousand dollars," he said, ". . . or more."

I closed my eyes and sank back against my pillow. Two hundred and fifty thousand dollars—when we barely had enough to pay the grocery bills. And even if we had the money, I was so traumatized by just the thought of surgery that I couldn't imagine going through it. Plus I had a history of health problems—ulcers, allergic reactions, unusual complications after other medical procedures—that didn't bode well for *any* operation, much less highly complicated ones.

"What happens if I don't have the surgery, Bob?" I asked. "I'll die, won't I?"

Bob didn't answer. Instead he moved onto the edge of my bed and put his arms around me. But I barely felt them. *This is it,* I thought. *The end of my life.* And the end of a year filled with one devastating event after another.

The past year in Houston had been terrible for us. Oil prices had plunged and Bob had been laid off from his job on an offshore oil rig. He'd been looking for work steadily, but nothing had come up. In the meantime his unemployment checks had stopped and our savings had dwindled away.

Next came the news that Bob's mother had Alzheimer's disease and his father had a malignant tumor. Bob and I moved in with Mom and Pop to care for them. Foolish as it was, we put off getting health insurance; we didn't have a cent to spare, and Bob would be getting a job any day now. Or so we thought.

I too was in a downward spiral of sinking spirits and increasing health problems. And then this! When I awoke one morning in late November my right leg and arm were strangely "asleep," and my mouth couldn't form the words I wanted to say. I managed to throw myself out of bed and into the hall, but then I collapsed. I was rushed to the hospital.

For two weeks I couldn't talk or communicate. I had never been so frightened. I went through a series of exhausting tests— and now Bob was at my side telling me the results:

Without the money, no operation.

Without the operation, no life.

"Then I'll just die," I said.

His arms tightened around me. But I pulled away. As much as I loved him, I wanted him to leave. "Go home," I said. "You need the rest." Inside of me the message was different: *I'm going to die. Go away. Leave me alone.*

Slowly he pulled on his jacket. After he left, the room was silent. *Thank goodness the other bed is empty,* I thought. I couldn't stand to have anybody else near me.

There was the squish of rubber-soled shoes in the corridor. I turned my head to see a wheelchair roll in, pushed by a smiling nurse. "Good news, Mrs. Gettle. You're getting company," she said.

A roommate! That was all I needed. I watched grudgingly as a slender black woman was helped out of the chair and into the adjoining bed. She had a pleasant face framed by soft gray hair. "Hello," she said, looking over as the nurse adjusted her covers. "I'm Flossie."

"Hello," I said wearily.

"What are you here for?" Flossie's voice was warm and friendly, but I was in no mood for talking. Tersely I explained my physical condition.

"When are they going to fix you up?" Flossie asked.

Never, I thought to myself, choking back tears. "There are some problems," I said. "We can't afford the surgery." As the nurse turned to go, I asked her to pull the curtains around my bed. "I'd like some privacy," I said weakly.

The curtains rattled on their rod, then closed around me like a tent, and Flossie vanished out of sight behind them. Vaguely I heard some muffled conversation about a mysterious attack that Flossie had had that evening. Her husband had rushed her to the hospital, and she was being kept overnight for observation.

But I paid little attention to what was going on. I curled up in misery.

I'd always been a "Christian" person. My mother had been a minister, and I had gone through all the right motions and participated in all the right church activities. But what good had it all done?

I felt totally abandoned. How would my husband cope when I was gone? Who would take care of Mom and Pop? Fears swirled in terrifying profusion.

The words sounded in my mind, with every breath I took. *You'll die, you'll die, you'll die . . .*

I fell into a heavy, churning sleep . . .

"Mrs. Gettle, wake up!" A voice called me; a hand was shaking my shoulder gently but firmly. The curtains that shrouded my bed had parted; a form leaned over me, silhouetted against the eerie glow of a small night-light in the corridor outside.

"What's wrong?" I mumbled.

"Nothing's wrong, honey," said a rich, gentle voice. "I have a message for you. From God."

From God? Flossie?

It *was* Flossie. She had left her own bed and was standing next to mine.

"I've been praying about you," she said, "and God spoke to me clear as a bell. He said, " 'Tell this lady I'm going to give her her surgery, and it's going to be successful.' " She patted my hand. "Now don't you worry about another thing. You'll *live.*"

With a tremble of the curtains, she was gone. I lay staring at the glowing hall light. The small clock on my bedside table said it was 2:30 in the morning, the middle of the night.

Abruptly I was filled with an overwhelming sense of peace. It was as if gentle hands had grasped my shoulders and turned me completely around. The hammering, negative voice in my head stopped. It was replaced with a fresher, calmer cadence. *You'll live, you'll live, you'll live . . .* I drifted back to sleep and slept better than I had in months.

The next morning I was released from the hospital. I was told that, short of having the necessary surgery, nothing further could be done for me. As I packed my things to go home, Flossie smiled knowingly from the next bed. "It will be all right, honey," she said with such conviction that it was impossible to doubt her. "God told me so."

Bob looked at me strangely as he drove me home. "It's good to see you so cheerful," he said. "Especially since you don't feel well."

Don't feel well? After months of illness and depression, I was feeling better and better. Instead of slumping down onto my bed the way I might have a few days before, I had the urge to get busy in the house, maybe even to check in with the neighbors to see what had happened since I'd been away.

You'll live. God will give you your surgery.

I saw my neighbor's car pass the window and pull into the driveway next door.

My neighbor, Dr. Howard Derman—I'd said hello to him over the fence, but that was all. But suddenly it hit me that he was a neurologist. He'd know more about what they told me in the hospital. I was out the door before my astonished husband could ask where I was going.

Dr. Derman was at his kitchen table having breakfast. I told him about my diagnosis and asked him to explain.

He drew on his napkin to illustrate. "There are two weak places in your arteries that bulge out," he explained. "If they aren't repaired, they can blow out, just like a weak spot on a tire." He went into more detail about the surgery, then asked who would be doing it.

"No one," I said. "We can't afford it."

He looked thoughtful for a moment, then began asking questions about Bob and me and our finances. "I'm affiliated with a local hospital," he said. On a previous visit there I'd been told I wasn't "destitute enough" to qualify for special assistance.

"It just seems to me," he went on, "that if ever two people needed special funding, it's you and Bob. Let me see what I can do."

It's hard to believe what happened next. Since my case was so unusual, the doctors asked if my operation could be filmed for teaching and research purposes, and the hospital would pay all charges. Is that what Flossie's incredible statement meant: "Tell this lady I'm going to *give* her her surgery"?

Bob couldn't get over how calm I was as they rolled me down toward the operating room, clutching a piece of paper bearing the words, *Let not your heart be troubled* (John 14:1).

I went through nearly nine hours of complicated surgery to repair the first aneurysm—and it all went smoothly. Within a few days I was up and walking in the halls. The doctors were amazed at my quick recovery. Ordinarily they would have sent me home for a few months to recover and regain my strength for the second operation, but I felt so strong and confident that I said, "Let's go ahead now."

Only thirteen days later I had another operation—and four days after that I was out of intensive care and walking around the wards, helping the nurses with some of their duties. No more lying around thinking about dying for me! The hospital staff could hardly believe it. When they commented on how well I was coping, I gave the explanation I'd given from the first.

"Oh," they said, laughing, "you're back to 'God gave me the surgery,' are you?" But I could tell they were impressed.

What turned me around—from a timid, fear-filled person to a confident, lively one? A lot of people would say it was the power of suggestion and I agree: God's suggestion, passed on by one of His faithful messengers and given to a desperate woman deep in despair in the middle of the night. How did that messenger happen to be in the bed next to mine that fateful night? That's one of the mysteries, for the doctors never found anything wrong with Flossie. She went home fine, and has stayed fine. I know, because Flossie and I have been fast friends ever since.

"When I woke you up that night," Flossie once said, "you must have wondered, 'What on earth's got into her?' "

And then she and I laughed, because we knew. It was nothing on earth.

Nothing on earth at all.

THE LONGEST WAIT OF MY LIFE
Mary Ann Fenyus

How well I remember the terrifying sense of aloneness that swept through me the day I knew for sure that I was going blind.

Not that I was surprised. I'd worn those awful thick glasses since I was twelve, and by themselves they caused me to feel isolated. No one wanted to play with the thin girl whose eyes were made beady by bottle-glass lenses.

But it wasn't until the spring of 1963, when I was twenty-nine years old and a teaching nun with the Sisters of St. Joseph, that the real blow fell. One morning I stood before my fifty wiggly first graders in St. Bernard's Parochial School just outside of Pittsburgh. The children were working on their A-B-Cs. I had made seven-inch-high paper cutout letters, pasted them on white showcards, and propped them up around the room. Big as the cutouts were, they were unrecognizable to me unless

I stood right next to them. So I memorized where key letters were. ABC in back of me. GHI to my right. MNO in front of me across the classroom.

On this morning one of the children in the back of the room missed a letter.

"Try again, Amy," I said.

The whole class started to titter. "I'm not *Amy,* Sister," a voice was saying from the blurred distance. "I'm *Bob!*"

Panic. I could no longer hide how bad my vision had become. That very day I started a round of visits to my superiors, desperately trying to see what could be done. The mother general sent me to see her own specialist, Dr. Jay Linn, Jr., of Pittsburgh. I was sitting now on the swivel stool in Dr. Linn's office, nervously fingering the sleeves of my black habit as he pulled back the slit lamp through which he had been examining the insides of my eyes.

"Yes, it is keratoconus, Sister," said Dr. Linn. "The cornea of your eye makes a cone instead of being rounded."

I tried to make Dr. Linn's face come into focus. "How bad is it, then?" My voice was barely audible.

"A few years ago you'd have gone blind. First your left eye; eventually your right." But then for the first time one word was spoken that gave me hope. *Transplant.* Today, Dr. Linn was saying, we can lift out the healthy cornea of a donor who has just died (age makes little difference) and insert it in the eye of a recipient.

"The key," Dr. Linn said, "is to find corneas. We have eye banks, but the term is misleading because there is no real bank of eyes you can draw on." A cornea apparently will perish in just a few hours, so surgeons constantly need new ones, and not enough people are making eye donations. "We have a long waiting list, Sister. But there's always a chance."

I signed up that very day and when I got back to the convent I packed a hospital bag with an extra nightgown, my bedcap, toothbrush, missal, and rosary. But a month went by. Two. Three. Four months passed. Vacation time came, and in June I moved to our Mother House in Baden, Pennsylvania, where the wait went on into mid-July. I would jump whenever a phone rang somewhere in the convent. But it was like my childhood all over again: the calls were never for me.

Meanwhile my eyes were getting progressively worse. Behind those ugly prism glasses I could hardly see out of my left eye, and my right wasn't much better. Heavy lines appeared beneath words when I tried to read. Then moved up *into* the words, making them almost impossible to interpret.

I was praying constantly during my long wait. So was my family in Beaver, Pennsylvania. So were the nuns who knew my situation. But unknown to me, another kind of prayer was being brought to bear—not one of words, but of deeds.

One day a few months earlier, on Easter Sunday, the assistant pastor at the Westminster Presbyterian Church in nearby Upper St. Clair Township told his congregation about the outcome of his own recent operation. He had regained his failing sight through corneal transplants. He urged his congregation to pledge eye donations to the local eye bank. One of the families who responded was the Gillilands, Will, June, and their five children, including a daughter named Julie, the second oldest, twelve years old. I had no idea of their existence then.

Now it was the night of July 17. Even though it was only nine o'clock, I was in my cell preparing for bed. We had to be up at 5:20 for Matins and Lauds, so it was lights out at ten, but there was no point in trying to read until then because the words on the page were all smudged now. I knelt on the hardwood floor in my white nightgown and white bedcap beside the brown bed in that little nine-by-twelve room, looking up at my crucifix. I prayed for a while, then turned back the sheet and crawled in.

Suddenly I had an intense feeling that someone was in danger. I sat upright. Had I been asleep—had a bad dream? What time was it? I turned on the light and struggled hard to read the clock on my nightstand. It was only 9:30.

At that moment my thin body gave a shudder. "Father, I'm just realizing! Before I can see again, someone has to die." But of course—that's why corneal recipients rarely knew who their donors were. The knowledge was too much to bear. I shuddered again. Out loud I quoted from the Requiem Mass. "Father," I said, "grant unto them eternal rest."

But why had I said *them?*

I lay in my narrow bed praying for unknown people in an

unknown situation. Yet, mysteriously, I was aware of my *connectedness* with them. I, who had been so alone, was in profound communion with people I would doubtless never meet. When I went to sleep I was still praying for them.

The convent's bells rang. Morning. I groped my way to chapel for Matins and Lauds. And all the while I went on praying, interceding for . . . for whom? For what?

A few hours later I heard a phone ring. Shortly the assistant mother general came running down the hall.

"The call's come through, Sister! They want you right away."

I didn't wait for the elevator. As fast as I dared, I made my way upstairs, grabbed my overnight bag, and within an hour was being admitted to the Pittsburgh Eye and Ear Hospital.

Dr. Linn told me he could let me have one cornea and would operate on my left eye. He bandaged my somewhat stronger right eye, then numbed my left with a local anesthetic, his soothing voice talking me through everything that was happening. About three hours into the operation, searing light smashed into my left eye. The new cornea was in place. I could see!

The ceiling. The operating-room lights. The outline of a nurse on my left side. Dr. Linn's hand near my face.

Everything was going perfectly, and yet, as I was returned to my hospital room, both eyes still bandaged, I continued to marvel at the experience I'd had a few hours earlier of "knowing" that someone was in danger.

My parents arrived as soon as I could have visitors. From behind my bandages I heard my mother's excited voice. "So, it's the best news! You are going to see!" We spent a happy time talking about the gift of sight. Then, pausing as if making a decision, Mother said, "I know who gave you her cornea."

"But that's not possible, Mother. The donor's name is a secret."

I heard the rattling of a newspaper. "There was a dreadful car accident last night. Half a family was killed: the father, his fifteen-year-old son and twelve-year-old daughter. When I was waiting for the elevator just now I heard hospital people talking. Your cornea belongs to the little girl. Her name is Julie."

As soon as I could, I wrote to the mother, June Gilliland. It was a confusing letter to write and I half expected Mrs. Gilliland never to answer. After all . . .

But by return mail came a letter, one that I could *read!*
Would I come to Upper St. Clair Township?

Which of course I did. I met June and her three small
daughters, each wearing her hair in long bangs. I found that I
was not at all shy. I seemed to know just what to say and soon
was urging June to talk about the night of the accident.

After a family picnic celebrating her husband's thirty-ninth
birthday, the Gillilands had returned home in two cars. Will
and all five of the children were in one automobile, while June
took her own mother home by another route. Will Gilliland—
a safety engineer by profession, a sensible man by nature—
always drove with care. The police pieced together the details.
A gray car, without lights, sped out of the night straight at
Will in Will's lane. The seventy-year-old driver of the other car
was drunk.

June for her part seemed to know just what to say to me too,
almost as if she were living inside my confusion. June told me
about Julie. I held her picture in my hand. Dark-haired. A good
student. Outgoing. Julie was twelve years old when she died,
the very age when I had last seen my childhood world clearly. I
spoke of my sense of guilt at knowing someone had to die before
I could see. Again, June knew just what to say. She took the
picture of Julie from my hands and spoke words that healed.
"Never forget," she said, looking at her child, "death is inevita-
ble, love is not."

Yes, that was true. In donating her eyes, Julie had chosen a
path of involvement. As June and I talked I glimpsed the hope
that my eyesight was just one part of a larger healing taking
place. I could see my physical world more clearly now, but there
was also a new insight into the world of the Spirit where my
tragedy is connected to others, my joy is others' too. In that
realm death and life touch each other.

Strange. Had I once before been to this universe, where all of us
are again connected, as perhaps we were in the beginning? I
remembered the night in my cell, the night of the accident. Into
my mind sprang the memory of sitting upright in bed, aware of
danger, struggling to read the face of the clock beside my bed.

"June . . ." I said, almost afraid to ask. "That night . . . did
the police fix the *time* of the accident?"

"Yes," June said. "We do know. It was 9:30."

❋ THE HEALING OF MAUDE BLANFORD

Catherine Marshall

Healing through faith remains a mystery to me. I have been part of prayer campaigns where it was gloriously granted, others where, at least in this world, it was not.

Why? There are no glib answers. Yet in my experience, as God has closed one door, He always opens another.

Last summer, a new friend from Louisville, Kentucky, opened a door on this difficult question by telling me of Maude Blanford's healing from terminal cancer eleven years ago. I was so intrigued that I flew to Louisville and got the details from Maude herself.

The woman across the dining table from me was a grandmotherly type, comfortable to be with. "How did your—ah, illness begin?" I asked, feeling foolish even asking the question to someone obviously in such radiant health.

"My left leg had been hurting me," Mrs. Blanford replied. "I thought it was because I was on my feet so much. Finally my husband and I decided that I should go to the doctor."

When her family doctor said words like "specialist" and "biopsy," the patient read the unspoken thought—malignancy.

Mrs. Blanford was referred to Dr. O. J. Hayes. He examined her on June 29, 1959, and prescribed radiation treatment. The treatment began July 7, and was followed by surgery on September 29. After the operation, when Mrs. Blanford pleaded with Doctor Hayes for the truth, he admitted, "It *is* cancer and it's gone too far. We could not remove it because it's so widespread. One kidney is almost nonfunctioning. The pelvic bone is affected—that's why you have the pain in your leg."

Maude Blanford was put on narcotics to control the by now excruciating pain and sent home to die. Over a six-month period, while consuming a thousand dollars' worth of pain-relieving drugs, she took stock of her spiritual resources and found them meager indeed. There was no church affiliation, no knowledge of the Bible, only the most shadowy concept of Jesus.

In January 1960, she suffered a cerebral hemorrhage and was rushed back to the hospital. For twelve days she lay unconscious. But Maude Blanford, oblivious to the world around her, was awake in a very different world. In her deep coma, a vivid image came to her. She saw a house with no top on it. The partitions between the rooms were there, the furniture in place, but there was no roof. She remembered thinking, *Oh, we must put a roof on it!*

When she came out of the coma, Mrs. Blanford's mind was very much intact, but bewildered. What could the roofless house have meant? As she puzzled over it, a Presence seemed to answer her. Today she has no hesitation in calling Him the Holy Spirit. "He seemed to show me that the house represented my body, but that without Jesus as my covering, my body had no protection."

From then until July 1960, her condition worsened. Heart action and breathing became so difficult, she was reduced to weak whispers. Even with drugs, the suffering became unbearable.

By July she knew she no longer had the strength to make the trip for radiation treatment. "On July first I told the nurse I wouldn't be coming back."

But that day, as her son-in-law helped her into the car outside the medical building, she broke down and wept. "At that moment I didn't want anything except for God to take me quickly—as I was. I said, 'God, I don't know who You are. I don't know anything about You. I don't even know how to pray. Just, Lord, have Your own way with me.' "

Though she did not realize it, Maude Blanford had just prayed one of the most powerful of all prayers—the prayer of relinquishment. By getting her own mind and will out of the way, she had opened the door to the Holy Spirit.

She did not have long to wait for evidence of His presence. Monday, July 4, dawned beautiful but hot. That afternoon Joe Blanford set up a cot for his wife outdoors under the trees. As the ill woman rested, into her mind poured some beautiful sentences.

"Is not this the fast that I have chosen? to loose the bands of wickedness, to undo the heavy burdens, and to let the oppressed go free . . .? Then shall thy light break forth . . . speedily. . . . Here I am."

I stared at Maude Blanford over the rim of my coffee cup. "But I thought you didn't know the Bible."

"I didn't! I'd never read a word of it. Only I knew this didn't sound like ordinary English. I thought, *Is that in the Bible?* And right away the words came: *Isaiah 58.* Well, my husband got a Bible for me. I had to hunt and hunt to find the part called Isaiah. But then when I found those verses just exactly as I had heard them—except for the last three words, 'Here I am'—well, I knew God Himself had really spoken to me!"

Over the next weeks Maude Blanford read the Bible constantly, often until two or three o'clock in the morning, seeing the Person of Jesus take shape before her eyes. As she read, a response grew in her, a response that is another of the Holy Spirit's workings in the human heart—praise. At home she began very slowly climbing the stairs, praising Jesus for each step she attained.

Next she tried putting a small amount of water in a pail. Sitting in a kitchen chair, she would mop the floor in the area immediately around her, scoot the chair a few inches, mop again. "Thank You, Jesus, for helping me do this!"

Her daughter-in-law, who was coming over almost daily to clean house for her, one day asked in great puzzlement, "Mom, how is it that your kitchen floor never gets dirty?"

The older woman smiled. "Well, I guess I'll have to confess—the Lord and I are doing some housework."

But their chief work, she knew, was not on this building of brick and wood, but on the house of her spirit, the house that had been roofless for so long. Gradually, as her knowledge of Him grew, she sensed His protective love surrounding and sheltering her. Not that all pain and difficulties were over. She was still on pain-numbing narcotics, still experiencing much nausea from the radiation.

One Saturday night, when the pain would not let her sleep, she lay on her bed praising God and reading the Bible. About 2:00 A.M., she drifted off to sleep with the Bible lying on her stomach. She felt that she was being carried to Heaven, traveling a long way through space. Then came a Voice out of the universe, "My child, your work is not finished. You are to go back." This was repeated three times, slowly, majestically.

The rest of the night she remained awake, flooded with joy, thanking God. When her husband woke up in the morning, she told him, "Honey, Jesus healed me last night."

She could see that he did not believe it; there was no change in her outward appearance. "But I knew I was healed and that I had to tell people." That very morning she walked to the Baptist church across the highway from their home and asked the minister if she could give a testimony. He gave permission, and she told the roomful of people that God had spoken to her in the night and healed her.

A few weeks later she insisted on taking a long bus trip to visit her son in West Virginia. Still on narcotics, still suffering pain, she nonetheless knew that the Holy Spirit was telling her to rely from now on on Jesus instead of drugs. At five o'clock on the afternoon of April 27, 1961, on the return bus journey, as she popped a pain-killing pill into her mouth at a rest stop, she knew it would be the last one.

So it turned out. In retrospect, physicians now consider this sudden withdrawal as great a miracle as the transformation of cancer cells to healthy tissue.

It took time to rebuild her body-house—nine months for her bad leg to be near normal, two years for all symptoms of cancer to vanish. When she called Doctor Hayes in 1962 over some small matter he almost shouted in astonishment. "Mrs. Blanford! What's happened to you! I thought you were—"

"You thought I was long since gone," she said, laughing.

"Please come to my office at once and let me examine you! I've got to know what's happened."

"But why should I spend a lot of money for an examination when I'm a perfectly well woman?" she asked.

"Mrs. Blanford, I promise you, this one is on us!" What the doctor found can best be stated in his own words: "I had lost contact with Mrs. Blanford and had assumed that this patient had expired. In May of 1962 she appeared in my office. It had been two-and-a-half years since her operation and her last X ray had been in July 1960 . . . . The swelling of her leg was gone. She had full use of her leg; she had no symptoms whatsoever, and on examination I was unable to ascertain whether or not any cancer was left . . . .

"She was seen again on November 5, 1962, at which time her examination was completely negative . . . . She has been seen periodically since that time for routine examinations . . . . She is absolutely asymptomatic . . . . This case is most unusual in that this woman had a proven, far-advanced metastatic cancer of the cervix and there should have been no hope whatsoever for her survival."

No hope whatsoever . . . No hope except the hope on which our faith is founded.

The miracle of Maude Blanford reminds me again of that scene on the night before His crucifixion when Jesus spoke quietly to His despairing disciples, "Ye have not chosen me, but I have chosen you" (John 15:16). He is still saying that to us today, while His Spirit—always working through human beings—sometimes confounds us, often amazes us, and is always the Guide to the future who can bring us joy and excited fulfillment.

GOD

Removes

THE STING OF DEATH

When the perishable puts on the imperishable, and the mortal puts on immortality, then shall come to pass the saying that is written:
   "Death is swallowed up in victory."
   "O death, where is thy victory?
   O death, where is thy sting?"
   . . . Thanks be to God, who gives us the victory through our Lord Jesus Christ.
                              —1 CORINTHIANS 15:54–57, RSV

MISSING
—*Author Unknown*

When the anxious hearts say "Where?"
He doth answer "In My care."

"Is it life or is it death?"
"Wait," He whispers. "Child, have faith!"

"Were they frightened at the last?"
"No, the sting of death is past."

"Did a thought of 'Home-Love' rise?"
"I looked down through Mother-eyes."

"Saviour, tell us, where are they?"
"In My keeping, night and day."

"Tell us, tell us, how it stands."
"None shall pluck them from My Hands."

RETURN FROM TOMORROW
Dr. George C. Ritchie, Jr.

When I was sent to the base hospital at Camp Barkeley, Texas, early in December 1943, I had no idea I was seriously ill. I'd just completed basic training, and my only thought was to get on the train to Richmond, Virginia, to enter medical school as part of the army's doctor-training program. It was an unheard-of break for a private, and I wasn't going to let a chest cold cheat me out of it.

But days passed and I didn't get better. It was December 19 before I was moved to the recuperation wing, where a jeep was to pick me up at 4:00 A.M. the following morning to drive me to the railroad station.

A few more hours and I'd make it! Then about 9:00 P.M. I began to run a fever. I went to the ward boy and begged some aspirin.

Despite the aspirin, my head throbbed, and I'd cough into the pillow to smother the sounds. At 3:00 A.M. I decided to get up and dress.

The next half-hour is a blur for me. I remember being too weak to finish dressing. I remember a nurse coming to the room, and then a doctor, and then a bell-clanging ambulance ride to the X ray building. Could I stand, the captain was asking, long enough to get one picture? I struggled unsteadily to my feet.

The whir of the machine is the last thing I remember.

When I opened my eyes, I was lying in a little room I had never seen before. A tiny light burned in a nearby lamp. For a while I lay there, trying to recall where I was. All of a sudden I sat bolt upright. The train! I'd miss the train!

Now, I know that what I am about to describe will sound incredible. I do not understand it any more than I ask you to; all that I can do is relate the events of that night as they occurred. I sprang out of bed and looked around the room for my uniform. Not on the bedrail: I stopped, staring. Someone was lying in the bed I had just left.

I stepped closer in the dim light, then drew back. He was dead. The slack jaw, the gray skin were awful. Then I saw the ring. On his left hand was the Phi Gamma Delta fraternity ring I had worn for two years.

I ran into the hall, eager to escape the mystery of that room. Richmond, that was the all-important thing—getting to Richmond. I started down the hall for the outside door.

"Look out!" I shouted to an orderly bearing down on me. He seemed not to hear, and a second later he had passed the very spot where I stood as though I had not been there.

It was too strange to think about. I reached the door, went through, and found myself in the darkness outside, speeding toward Richmond. Running? Flying? I only know that the dark earth was slipping past while other thoughts occupied my mind, terrifying and unaccountable ones. The orderly had not seen me. What if the people at medical school could not see me either?

In utter confusion I stopped by a telephone pole in a town by a large river and put my hand against the guy wire. At least the wire *seemed* to be there, but my hand could not make contact with it. One thing was clear: in some unimaginable way I had lost my firmness of flesh, the hand that could grip that wire, the body that other people saw.

I was beginning to know too that the body on that bed was mine, unaccountably separated from me, and that my job was to get back and rejoin it as fast as I could.

Finding the base and the hospital again was no problem. Indeed, I seemed to be back there almost as soon as I thought of it. But where was the little room I had left? So began what must have been one of the strangest searches ever to take place: the search for myself. As I ran from one ward to the next, past room after room of sleeping soldiers, all about my age, I realized how unfamiliar we are with our own faces. Several times I stopped by a sleeping figure that was exactly as I imagined myself. But the fraternity ring, the Phi Gam ring, was lacking, and I would speed on.

At last I entered a little room with a single dim light. A sheet had been drawn over the figure on the bed, but the arms lay along the blanket. On the left hand was the ring.

I tried to draw back the sheet, but I could not seize it. And now that I had found myself, how could one join two people who were so completely separate? And there, standing before this problem, I thought suddenly: *This is death. This is what we human beings call "death," this splitting up of one's self.* It was the first time I had connected death with what had happened to me.

In that most despairing moment, the little room began to fill with light. I say "light," but there is no word in our language to describe brilliance that intense. I must try to find words, however, because incomprehensible as the experience was to my intellect, it has affected every moment of my life since then.

The light which entered that room was Christ. I knew because a thought was put deep within me: *You are in the presence of the Son of God.* I have called Him "light," but I could also have said "love," for that room was flooded, pierced, illuminated, by total compassion. It was a presence so comforting, so joyous and all-satisfying, that I wanted to lose myself forever in the wonder of it.

But something else was present in that room. With the presence of Christ (simultaneously, though I must tell it one by one), there also had entered every single episode of my entire life. There they were, every event and thought and conversation, as palpable as a series of pictures. There was no first or last, each one was contemporary, each one asked a single question, *What did you do with your time on earth?*

I looked anxiously among the scenes before me: school, home, scouting, and the cross-country track team—a fairly typical boyhood, yet in the light of that presence it seemed a trivial and irrelevant existence.

I searched my mind for good deeds.

Did you tell anyone about Me? came the question.

I didn't have time to do much, I answered. *I was planning to, then this happened. I'm too young to die!*

No one, the thought was inexpressibly gentle, *is too young to die.*

And now a new wave of light spread through the room, already so incredibly bright, and suddenly we were in another world. Or rather, I suddenly perceived all around us a very different world occupying the same space. I followed Christ through ordinary streets and countrysides, and everywhere I saw this other existence strangely superimposed on our familiar world.

It was thronged with people. People with the unhappiest faces I ever have seen. Each grief seemed different. I saw businessmen walking the corridors of the places where they had worked, trying vainly to get someone to listen to them. I saw a mother following a sixty-year-old man, her son I guessed, cautioning him, instructing him. He did not seem to be listening.

Suddenly I was remembering myself, that very night, caring about nothing but getting to Richmond. Was it the same for these people; had their hearts and minds been all concerned with earthly things, and now, having lost earth, were they still fixed hopelessly here? I wondered if this was hell: to care most when you are most powerless.

I was permitted to look at two more worlds that night—I cannot say "spirit worlds" for they were too real, too solid. Both were introduced the same way: a new quality of light, a new openness of vision, and suddenly it was apparent what had been there all along. The second world, like the first, occupied this very surface of the earth, but it was a vastly different realm. Here was no absorption with earthly things, but—for want of a better word—with truth.

I saw sculptors and philosophers here, composers and inventors. There were universities and great libraries and scientific laboratories that surpass the wildest inventions of science fiction.

Of the final world I had only a glimpse. Now we no longer seemed to be on earth, but immensely far away, out of all relation to it. And there, still at a great distance, I saw a city— but a city, if such a thing is conceivable, constructed out of light. At that time I had not read the Book of Revelation, nor, incidentally, anything on the subject of life after death. But here was a city in which the walls, houses, streets seemed to give off light, while moving among them were beings as blindingly bright as the One who stood beside me. This was only a moment's vision, for the next instant the walls of the little room closed around me, the dazzling light faded, and a strange sleep stole over me . . .

To this day, I cannot fully fathom why I was chosen to return to life. All I know is that when I woke up in the hospital bed in that little room, in the familiar world where I'd spent all my life, it was not a homecoming. The cry in my heart that moment has been the cry of my life since: Christ, show me Yourself again.

It was weeks before I was well enough to leave the hospital, and all that time one thought obsessed me: to get a look at my chart. At last I was left unattended; there it was in terse medical shorthand: Pvt. George Ritchie, died December 20, 1943, double lobar pneumonia.

Later I talked to the doctor who had signed the report. He told me there was no doubt in his mind that I was dead when he examined me, but nine minutes later the soldier who had been assigned to prepare me for the morgue came running to him to ask him to give me a shot of adrenalin. The doctor gave me a hypo of adrenalin directly into the heart muscle, all the while disbelieving what his own eyes were seeing. My return to life, he told me, without brain damage or other lasting effect, was the most baffling circumstance of his career.

Today I feel that I know why I had the chance to return to this life. It was to become a physician so that I could learn about man and then serve God. And every time I have been able to serve our God by helping some brokenhearted adult, treating some injured child, or counseling some teenager, then deep within I have felt that He was there beside me again.

RECITAL FOR ONE

Phyllis M. Letellier

My husband and I had been farming just a few years up to the summer our sons were two and four years old. We were trying hard to get established, so my husband still worked full time off the farm. My days were full—driving a tractor to do field work, tending livestock, trying to be a good homemaker and mother. But at one point there came a welcome lull in my labors. A good chance to get away.

I loaded the boys in our ten-year-old car and drove all the way across Wyoming to visit my parents for a few days. We arrived exhausted, and so my bedtime prayers were a quick "Thank You for a safe trip" and the usual "Please, dear Lord, be with me tomorrow."

The next afternoon, Grandma was pleased to have her only grandsons all to herself in the kitchen. And for me, here was a rare opportunity: time to indulge my love of piano playing.

I had brought a pile of long-neglected sheet music with me: my favorites and some I knew my father would enjoy. Shortly after I began to play, Father came in and sat in a living-room chair near the piano. He listened a minute, then pointed to a book on the music rack and said, "Play something out of that."

My father was a longtime fan of the Lawrence Welk television show, and the book he indicated was a collection of ragtime songs arranged by Tiny Little, who played piano on the show in its early days. Ragtime was my favorite kind of music and I'd had the book for several years. I had tried diligently to learn the songs, but with little formal training and even less natural ability, I hadn't been very successful.

I played the one song in the book that, with a lot of effort, I had mastered, and then I started to set the book aside. I knew the other songs were beyond my skill.

"Oh, play another one," said Father.

I looked through the book. Perhaps there was one other song I might be able to bluff my way through. I tried it and found I could play it almost perfectly, surely the best I'd ever done. Surprised and encouraged, I tried one more song . . . and then another, until I'd played—passably—the whole ragtime book.

My father enjoyed my ragtime recital, enjoyed it in a quiet

way. I could tell he was feeling tired, but I didn't realize at the time that he wasn't feeling well. There was no way for me to know the shock that lay ahead. My father died of heart failure the next morning.

I was where I needed to be for the next week, and when I returned home after Father's funeral I was tired and sad. But I had to resume the farm chores, and maybe that was just as well, for the work took my mind off my sorrow.

Finally, a few weeks later, I found time for a few minutes of recreational piano playing. I dug out the ragtime book, thinking, *Now that I know all these songs, I'll just play straight through this book.* I first played the one song I'd always been able to play. Then I went on to the other familiar one. I didn't play it very well. And how about the rest of the songs, the ones I'd sailed through that last afternoon with Father? Well, those songs were once again as far beyond me as they'd always been, my fingers utterly incapable of playing the notes my eyes were reading.

You might think this sudden return to incompetence would have saddened me. But it didn't. Instead, I felt consoled, even happy. Clearly God had given me a momentary gift, the chance to play gladdening songs for my father in his final hours. I closed the ragtime book and put it back in the piano bench, knowing more than ever that God is loving and kind.

I SAW ERICA RUNNING
Linda Hanick

Our daughter, Erica, came into this world blind. Later, grave medical problems followed. Erica was almost four when it became clear she was dying. As Jack and I kept vigil at her hospital bedside, our prayers for her healing gradually became prayers for wisdom and acceptance.

Then Jack looked at me searchingly. "Linda," he said, "we should do more than pray to God about Erica. We need to talk to Erica about God."

I knew he was right. Erica was afraid, afraid of dying.

Despite her pain, I sensed she was holding on to us because we were the surest love she knew.

Cupping her tiny hands, we told her that God's love was so much greater than ours, and that she had to try to let go—of this hospital room, this bed, even us.

"Where you are going is a safe place, more beautiful and full of love than anything you've ever known . . ."

In my mind I saw Erica running, skipping over emerald grass through fields of rainbow-colored flowers. Her golden hair blazed in the sunlight. Her voice was laughter, and her eyes were like the sky, cloudless and blue. She was no longer blind.

A nurse came by to record Erica's vital signs. Though it was clear Erica's physical condition remained the same, I sensed a change, something deep in her spirit.

I was about to tell Jack when he said, "You know, just before the nurse came in I had the strongest image. I saw Erica, so vividly, skipping and running across a field of beautiful flowers. She was laughing. And her eyes were clear and blue as the sky."

THE AWAKENING
Michelle Yates

During the early morning hours of a warm night in June 1987, I was asleep in our home when something caused me to awaken. At first I thought I was dreaming. But no, I was sure I was awake, and still I heard it. Music. Beautiful, melodic strumming. I got up to check if someone had left a radio or TV on, but that wasn't it. I looked in on our four children to see if any of them was up playing a record. But all were sound asleep—except for our two-year-old, Jeriel, who was staring out the window.

"Jeriel, what are you doing?"

He turned toward me, his blue eyes wide. "Mommy, I hear songs."

I crouched down by his curly blond head and looked out the window, but I saw nothing, just the leaves on the tree. I picked him up. "Sweetheart, I hear it too. But let's try to go back to sleep." As I carried him back to bed and plumped up his Donald Duck pillow, my heart pounded. What *was* it?

Back in our bedroom I woke my husband, Michael. "Do you hear the music?" I asked. Groggily he shook his head and was soon snoring again.

The beautiful strumming became louder. Then it stopped, and a lively high-pitched voice began to sing, coming from the direction of our fenced-in, above-ground swimming pool. I clearly heard the words:

> *In all things give Him praise,*
> *In all your days give Him your praise.*
> *He alone is worthy of your praise.*
> *Though you be racked with pain,*
> *Still proclaim He is Lord*
> *And give Him praise . . .*

Next morning, as bright sunshine filled the house, and Mike went off to his job as an electronics engineer at the Highland Park Chrysler plant, I wondered if it had been a dream. Then as I poured cornflakes, Jeriel asked, "Mommy, who was that singing last night?"

I caught my breath, my mind whirling. Jeriel was soon rolling his little car across the breakfast table, but I continued to wonder. The message had sounded like what I'd always thought the singing of angels would be, and I've always believed in angels, God's messengers. But if it was indeed the music of angels, what could it mean? Jeriel and I were the only ones, apparently, who had heard anything. I just didn't know what to make of the strange experience.

Two months later, on Wednesday, August 19, 1987, Jeriel was so wound up that he didn't want to nap. Always a climber, he was up on the sofa back, then on my kitchen counters. Finally he crawled next to me on my bed, laid his head on my chest, and then looked up. "Game, Mommy." It was a little amusement we enjoyed. I pointed to his eye and said, "Eye, eye," then to his nose, "nose, nose," and on to his mouth, teeth, and cheeks. I brushed my fingers through his soft blond curls and he laughed. Then, as always, I ended by saying, "Mommy loves you, Jeriel; Jesus loves you." He kissed me and said, "Jerielly loves you, and Jesus loves you too."

He relaxed and, looking at the picture over my bed, whispered, "Mommy, that's Jesus." I was thrilled. I had been trying to teach him that for months.

At supper Jeriel was the clown as usual. He had learned a new giggle, and all of us had fun in our attempts to mimic him. Afterward, the children asked to go swimming. I wasn't feeling well, so Mike said he would watch them while I rested on the sofa. Soon I dozed off.

Suddenly I was wakened. "Mommy, Jeriel fell in the pool!" It was six-year-old Athena, her eyes wide in terror.

I leapt up and raced out the back door. There on the pool's wooden deck Jeriel lay wet and motionless. Mike was bending over him, frantically giving him CPR. "Call the police!" Mike yelled.

In minutes, Mike and our landlord, who lives nearby, were putting Jeriel into our van to rush him to the Saline Hospital. Before leaving, Mike brokenly explained that while he was in the basement getting some toys, he hadn't noticed that Jeriel had slipped out of the house and climbed the pool fence.

Athena, five-year-old Gabriel, and three-year-old Josiah were crying. "Jerielly is dead!" screamed Athena. "I don't want my baby brother to be dead!"

"We don't know that," I soothed. Then I sat them down. "Look, Jeriel is in the hands of God. We must trust Him. Now let's pray for Jeriel to be strong. We are a family, and must stay together in Jesus, no matter what."

I put our children in the care of neighbors and rushed to the hospital. There Mike and I waited, gripping each other's hands.

When the doctor appeared, her face was grave. "We finally got a faint heartbeat," she said. "But"—she touched my shoulder—"you must remember, there may be some brain damage."

"I don't care," I cried. "I just want my baby back alive."

Finally they let us see Jeriel. He was lying in the trauma room with machines beeping. I brushed wet curls from his closed eyes. How small and helpless he looked. Soon a helicopter came to whisk him to Mott Hospital in Ann Arbor, which the doctor said was the best pediatric center in the area.

Mike went home for Jeriel's Donald Duck pillow and his favorite shirt and pants, for Jeriel to wear when he came home.

Then we waited at Mott Hospital. I felt as if I were in a bad dream, and I kept asking God, "Please, wake me up."

Finally, the doctor came out. "Your son is in a deep coma. His brain has been without oxygen long enough to suffer damage. To what extent we don't know."

Mike and I turned and held each other, and prayed. Friends and relatives came to sit with us and pray. I sensed God's sweet Holy Spirit surrounding us all.

Two days later the doctor came in with Jeriel's test results. "It's not promising," he said. "Your son is ninety percent brain dead. He might live on or die in a few days or weeks. We can't tell."

I began sobbing. My friend Glenda put her arm around me. "Michelle, you have to give Jeriel to Jesus."

I stared at her. *No,* I thought, *God has turned things around before for me. He can heal Jeriel too.* Later that day as I held Jeriel's hand and talked to him, he drew my hand up to his heart. My spirits soared. He could hear me!

But every report was worse than the one before. On Sunday night, after Jeriel had been in a coma for four days, the doctor offered no hope. "It could be," he said, "that the time may soon come when we should turn off his life-support system." He looked up at us gravely. "We could keep him going, or do you want us just to let him go? We will need to know your decision soon."

Mike felt it would be best to let Jeriel go but I could not think of it.

Rachel, one of the many friends who had comforted us, stayed with me in the waiting room that night. I took off my shoes, lay down on a chair that converted into a bed, and finally went to sleep. But then I dreamed that I rose from my bed and walked into Jeriel's room. His body was attached to all sorts of needles and tubes. I leaned over and whispered in his ear, "Jeriel, my little sweetheart, I have always tried to teach you to obey Mommy and Daddy. Well, now there is another who is calling you. I told you that above all others we are to obey our Heavenly Father. And if He is calling you, you must go to Him."

I picked up my child, and to my surprise, all the needles and tubes fell from him. I cradled his limp body in my arms. As I stood crying, I heard someone call my name. I looked up. It was Jesus! His eyes were full of compassion.

"O Father, heal him, please, whether it be by his living or going home with You," I begged. But I already knew the answer. "Father," I continued, "when Jeriel was born, we dedicated him to You. He is Yours. I have always prayed that Your will be done."

He smiled. "Daughter, I love you and will give you strength and comfort."

I held Jeriel close, kissed him, and laid him at Jesus' feet. I stepped back and the Lord picked him up. Instantly Jeriel awoke. He looked up at the Lord, grinned, and said, "Hi, Jesus!"

The Lord held Jeriel out to me, and once more we played our little game. I touched his ear, his eye, his nose, mouth, and cheeks, and finished as always by saying, "Mommy loves you; Jesus loves you." He kissed me and said, "Jerielly loves you, and Jesus loves you too."

Then Jesus, with Jeriel in His arms, began to walk out of the room. The Lord motioned me to come. We walked along the darkened hospital corridor, took the elevator down to the lobby, and went past the reception desk to the double glass doors of the hospital entrance. Outside, instead of the courtyard, there was a hill covered with deep green grass, and the sky was pure and clear.

I stood inside the door, watching in awe as Jesus set Jeriel down. He took off in a run for the hill, stopped, picked a flower, and counted the petals, his voice crystal clear: "One, two, three, nine!" (He still hadn't learned to count.) "See," Jesus said to me, "he is alive. All who are in My care are alive and growing here."

Then He and Jeriel walked over the hill together. Once, Jeriel looked back, smiled, and called, "Mommy, I love you and will always be at your side." Then they were gone and I went back to sleep on my makeshift bed in the waiting room.

In the morning when I awoke, Rachel asked me a startling question: "Did you know you were walking in your sleep last night?" She went on to tell me I had left the room, walked down the corridor, and taken the elevator.

"I couldn't have," I insisted.

"No," she said, "you did some walking all right." Rachel
pointed to my feet. "Okay, then explain why your shoes are on.
You took them off when you went to bed. Now each is on the
wrong foot."

I looked down. She was right.

Then the night nurse stuck her head into the room and said
to me, "I hope I didn't disturb you last night—when you were
in Jeriel's room, praying."

I was stunned. I had thought it all a dream. And yet . . .

Had it been only two months since I'd wondered if I'd had
another dream—the music of the angels? But that music had
been real. I had heard it. Jeriel had heard it. Why? Now,
looking back, I knew. God was preparing us. But last night? It
must have been the hand of God as well.

I got up and went into Jeriel's room, now half expecting to
find his bed empty. But he was there, still connected to the
tubes and the hissing machine. Yet something was different. As
I looked down at him, somehow Jeriel was the same. Then I
knew: Jeriel was gone; only his body lived on.

From that moment on I was at ease. I did not have to insist
on keeping his life-support system running; I could let go.

But Mike and I didn't have to make that decision. In forty-
eight hours Jeriel's heart stopped beating. And for the first time
since the accident, he was smiling.

❄ EVERYTHING WILL BE ALL RIGHT
Ruth Whittet

When the doctor told us Jim had cancer, we could hardly grasp
the words. This was something that just didn't happen to young
marrieds, certainly not to *us!* It couldn't happen to a strong,
healthy young man just beginning a productive life—not to a
father of three small children.

But in some numbing, inexplicable way it had, and as Jim
and I began to take it in, we did what I suppose most people do
at such times—we turned to God in panic. Up till then we'd
made feeble attempts to attend church, never really settling on

one denomination, but trying first one and then another. Now in real earnest we began to explore spiritually—studying, praying, reading the Bible together.

One night I lay in bed beside my sleeping husband, unable to stop my thoughts. The house was dark and still, the children peacefully asleep. Through a crack under the window shade the stars were visibly twinkling in the sky. And I lay there cold with fear. My sweet, gentle, handsome young husband was going to die. "O God, help us, help him, help me to help him. Give us a miracle, Lord," I prayed.

And there, in the upper left corner of the room, the miracle began. It was a ball of light, whirling, coming closer, brighter and brighter, showering sparks around the room like a Fourth of July sparkler, moving, but with a powerful stillness like God's universe.

Blinking, I sat up in bed and still the light was there. Then I heard the words, tremendous and gentle as the light that seemed now to fill the house.

"Everything will be all right."

Five words, but somehow I knew that God Himself had spoken them.

Often in the following two years those words were all I had to hang onto. For in spite of repeated surgery and radiation treatments, Jim—to the outward eye anyway—was growing worse, the pain ever harder to bear, the once tall, strong body thin and wasted.

Then came that special night. For three days past, with every waking breath Jim had begged me to help in withstanding the pain. Now at last he was sleeping peacefully. But, exhausted as I was, somehow I couldn't go to bed.

The children were afraid but very perceptive. They did everything quietly and with an understanding obedience that said, "We know what's happening and will not add to the upset." After kissing their daddy and me goodnight, they had gone quickly to sleep without the usual rituals of the bedtime story and trips to the bathroom.

Some months before, we had moved Jim's bed to the living room. As I sat beside him there, watching him breathing regularly, his pleading voice quieted, I felt a wonderful sense of peace. Once again, as I had so many times in the last two years, I seemed to hear those words, "Everything will be all right."

Still I did not go to my own bed in the next room but sat beside him, silently reading the Bible and praying. I wanted so much to ask God to erase all of this, to let it be a bad dream. But it wasn't a dream. It was stubbornly, horribly real.

Finally, after two hours of praying, then sobbing, then reading, then hoping, then daring not to hope, I relinquished my hold on this person I loved more than anything else in the world. I said the prayer that I now believe gave my husband relief from his suffering: "O God, take him if You must, but don't let him suffer anymore." Then I kissed him, went into my room, and fell asleep immediately.

For several months preceding that night Jim had awakened me at three o'clock each morning to talk and pray with him. So it was habit, I suppose, that called me from sleep that night at 3:00 A.M. as usual. But it was what happened before I awoke that is so hard to put into words. For many years I didn't even try. Maybe I was selfish, wanting to hold onto it for myself, receiving comfort from it. Maybe I was afraid people would think me insane or self-deluding. But I have never been more certain of anything than of this event.

Suddenly I was wide awake instantly, as if my body were tensed for the unexpected. I lay there listening for any sound from the living room. I did not get up immediately but waited to absorb a Presence that once again seemed to fill the room. I looked around, expecting another bright light, for I felt the same exhilaration I had that other time. But there was no light, no voice. I lay there waiting and all at once I was remembering the dream I had just had. I closed my eyes and experienced the dream over again.

My husband's mother, who had passed away almost eight years before, and a good friend of the family, Aunt Charlotte, who had died some years before that, were standing in our living room. Together they looked down at the bed where my husband lay. They talked and laughed, joyously greeting their loved one. Although I couldn't hear their words, I understood they were telling Jim that they had come to take him home with them.

At first he seemed to be resisting; then just as easily and nonchalantly he nodded. By his acceptance he seemed to say that he knew he could no longer take care of his family, that he could leave them in God's hands. There was no more pain reflected on Jim's face. He got up, looked at the worn, pain-lined face of the body that was no longer his, took an arm of each woman, and together they left the house.

I rose from my bed and tiptoed to the door of the living room. Jim's body lay on the bed, strangely quiet.

There, in the silence of death, in a small house like thousands of other small houses in the world, I felt no sadness, no immediate grief, only humility and a sense of the reality of God. For He had visited me with His love and a promise, and had come again to show me the fulfillment—everything was all right, now and forever.

THE PHONE CALL
Linda A. Fuesz

Outside the bedroom window on this Sunday morning in July, the birds were just awaking. The air had the freshness that seems to exist only in those moments before the sun rises.

Inside, two people lay side by side. For forty years they had shared their lives and been attuned to each other, but never as intensely as now. For fourteen months, since the surgery that revealed the presence of cancer in his body, their marriage had taken on another dimension. The possibility that their time together on earth was drawing to a close made every moment precious.

She'd found herself studying his face when he wasn't aware of her presence. She wanted to memorize every feature: the eyes revealing the kindness inside the man, the large nose that the family lovingly teased him about, the mouth that smiled so easily or was so often pursed for whistling.

He'd been spending more hours lying on the couch or out in his hammock under a tree. Often he'd been lost in thought with a faraway look in his eyes. She longed to know what he was thinking, but to ask would be an intrusion on the thoughts which seemed to be one of the last things he could control as his body weakened.

She was in a deep sleep. He was beginning to stir. His first movements brought her quickly from her slumber, and she was immediately wide awake.

"Do you need some help?" she asked.

"No, I think I can take care of it," he replied as he reached for the urinal beside the bed. Lately, he'd not had the strength to walk down the hall to the bathroom when he awoke during the night.

After several minutes of fumbling, he admitted he would need her help after all.

"This is so ridiculous!" he said as they settled back into their warm bed. How difficult it was for him—indeed, for anyone—to have to depend on another for even the most basic needs.

"It's not at all ridiculous," she reassured him.

They were drifting off to sleep again. His arms were around her when suddenly he raised his head off the pillow and looked intently toward the east window of the bedroom.

"What is that bright light?" he asked, his voice intense.

She looked at him and then toward the window. "It's just the sun coming up."

"No, it's—"

He struggled to speak. His eyes showed that he'd seen something he wanted to tell her about, but he could not bring out the words. At that moment he drifted into unconsciousness.

Was this the moment she had been fearing? Quickly making sure he was carefully covered up, she slipped out of bed, reached for her robe, and climbed the stairs to the bedroom where their youngest son and his wife were sleeping. The doctor was telephoned, then their youngest daughter and her husband, who lived a short distance away.

The doctor confirmed what they had sensed already, that he had only hours to live.

The hours passed. The members of the family took turns sitting at the side of his bed. Even though he was in a coma, they felt that he would sense their presence and their love. It was she who was there beside him when the telephone in the hall rang. It rang again. Everyone else seemed to be in a different part of the house. Though the family had protected her from calls that morning, she knew she must answer this one. She picked up the phone just as the others were rounding the corner to answer for her.

"Hello?" she said.

On the other end a small, weak voice said, "Don't be afraid—the Lord's blessings are with you."

Her mind raced as she searched her memory trying to identify the strange voice. She was unable to respond because there was something so odd about the call. The look on her face was one of confusion as she held out the phone to her son-in-law.

"Hello?" he spoke into the receiver. Then he turned to her. "There's no one there now. Who was it, Mother?"

"I don't know, dear. It was a voice that sounded weak, far away, strange."

As the phone was replaced on its cradle, her daughter-in-law was the first to ask, "Did you see it, Mother? Did you see the phone? Did you see the phone glowing?"

And surely, they had all witnessed the strange phenomenon. There they were, a wife and mother of forty years surrounded by members of her family; a statistician with a master's degree, a statistician with a bachelor's degree, a plant pathologist with a doctoral degree, and a businessman, all standing in the dim hallway by the golden wall-phone. The very moment she had handed the phone to her son-in-law, the glowing had ceased and the caller was gone.

The glowing phone with the strange message did not change the course of the morning. When the moment of death came a few hours later, she was sitting, once again, at his side. She was watching the slow pulsing artery in his neck when the pulsing simply stopped. She remained near when the doctor pronounced death, and then she went downstairs to the basement. To watch her husband leave home for the last time was more than she could bear.

It has been seven years since that morning in July. I share this story with you today as an encouragement. You see, the man who died was my father. And my mother, who had so dreaded his death and was frightened by what life would be like without him, walked gallantly through the difficult days when her family returned to their own homes and their own lives. The two-story family home which she'd been sure would never offer her comfort without her husband became a place of solace and refuge after all. She never experienced any fear of staying alone. Mother immediately took over the upkeep of the yard, the

house, the car, the finances, all duties which Daddy had performed and in which she had taken little interest. She not only
handled these things, but accomplished them with skill and
with a rewarding sense of fulfillment as well.

I believe that Mother was changed and strengthened by the
mysterious voice on the glowing telephone.

And we, her children, have observed with amazement and
humble thanksgiving how faithful the Lord is to His children
when they are in need. We will not know until we meet the
Lord face to face what wonderful bright light my father was
seeing just before he lost consciousness. Nor will we know who
was on the other end of the glowing phone. Yet the words
"Don't be afraid—the Lord's blessings are with you" continue
to have their impact. Is it not possible that the Lord, who
understands every desire of our hearts, had compassion on my
mother and allowed my father a final phone call?

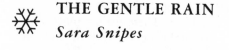

THE GENTLE RAIN
Sara Snipes

For Robert and me, rain was always heaven-sent. During our
courtship there was not much money for entertainment; however, we always enjoyed walking together—particularly in the
rain. The rain poured continually on our wedding day. For the
next twenty-one years of our marriage Robert often told of
stopping for gas in my little town of Watkinsville, Georgia, on
the way to our wedding. Since Robert was from south Georgia,
no one knew him. The owner of the gas station laughed and told
Robert about some poor nut who was getting married in this
downpour. Some poor nut indeed!

For our wedding, Robert had had an inscription engraved
inside my ring, but I didn't know how it read until I removed
the ring as he checked us into our honeymoon suite. There I saw
the words, *Because You Walked With Me in the Rain.*

Through the years of child rearing, losing parents through
death, moving, and worrying about jobs—no matter the
problem—our faith in God remained steadfast, and we always

took comfort in His word, just like it says, "My words shall fall upon you like the gentle rain" (Deuteronomy 32:2, TLB).

Then one night Robert died suddenly from a heart attack. Soon family and friends gathered around me, but after they left, I didn't want to go to bed. I felt so alone. I wandered outside and stood on the front porch. The night was quiet, the sky was clear. And then, for only a few remarkable seconds, there came the familiar, comforting, reassuring sound—of raindrops splattering on the sidewalk before me.

WHEN I SAW HEAVEN IN MOTHER'S EYES
Julia Tinkey

There's something about a hospital in the dead of night that is different from anything else—muted sighs and stirrings, the light from the nurses' station at the end of the floor.

I sat by Mother's bed, watching. There wasn't much else I could do. Jean Hudson, the night nurse, was in and out, checking Mother's pulse and blood pressure.

In fact, as the minutes crawled past, I grew more and more sensitive to the impulse that had made me leave my husband and our three children asleep and drive to the hospital at midnight. We'd known for six weeks that Mother was dying. Ever since surgery had revealed inoperable cancer, I'd spent part of each day at her side. This night I *had to be with her.*

It was true, the last few days she'd been failing rapidly, in much pain, drifting in and out of a coma. Several times the doctor had been on the verge of telling her that further treatment was useless—but we all hesitated. All her life Mother had been such an active person, teaching at the high school, running the farm, doing office work for dad's pulpwood business, raising five children, and cheerfully taking on jobs at church. To be able to fight now, however vainly, we felt was important to her.

She still had not moved nor opened her eyes since I arrived. I repeated again the prayer I had said so often in that room. It was that Mother not have to go with drugs numbing that close harmony of mind to mind and heart to heart we had always had in our family. As I had done daily the past six weeks, I prayed that Mother—who had served God so faithfully these seventy years—be allowed to come to Him in dignity and acceptance and peace.

"Julia!" Mother stirred on the bed. "Are you there, Julia?"

I assured her that I was, and she asked me to come closer. She wanted to apologize, she said, for having been so difficult (which of course she hadn't).

Her eyes opened; they looked straight into mine. "The doctor told me. And, Julia, it's all right. I've left it up to God. I'm in God's hands now, and it is so wonderful."

As she was saying this, she seemed bathed in light. As I stared at her, the mysterious radiance enveloped me as well; I felt as if I were drowning in the love and joy on her face.

I realized that she was smiling and I smiled back—but I could not express this awareness enough through smiles; it seemed that my body must burst with the fullness of that instant.

The instant stretched into minutes and the minutes into almost an hour as we looked at each other, exposed and filled with the living presence of God. I felt that Mother was seeing a world beyond the physical one, and that I was *almost* there with her.

I said to her, "Do you mean, Mother, that you see God?" and she answered, "Yes, Julia, face to face, and it is so important that everyone know. Tell Murray, Carol, Miriam, George," naming my brothers and sisters. "It's so wonderful!"

She seemed so alert, so like her former self that in frustration I almost shouted at her. "What's so wonderful? Tell me!"

"Millions and millions of people," she began slowly. "So many millions . . . and all on different levels. There's light . . . light everywhere . . . so much light!"

Her eyes seemed so full of love and they never left mine. Her voice remained strong as she continued. "Things get between us and God. Tell them all not to let things separate them from God. I've been so concerned with my own little problems and desires. Tell them, Julia—the glory of the Lord—it is wonderful!"

They were the last words that Mother spoke. Her eyes closed, but the smile did not fade.

PISGAH
—*Willard Wattles*

By every ebb of the river-side
My heart to God hath daily cried;
By every shining shingle-bar
I found the pathway of a star;
By every dizzy mountain height
He touches me for cleaner sight,
As Moses' face hath shined to see
His intimate divinity.
Through desert sand I stumbling pass
To death's cool plot of friendly grass,
Knowing each painful step I trod
Hath brought me daily home to God.

GOD

Orders

HIS ANGELS

For he orders his angels to protect you wherever you go. They will steady you with their hands to keep you from stumbling against the rocks on the trail.
—PSALM 91:11–12, TLB

NOW THE DAY IS OVER
—*Sabine Baring-Gould*

Now the day is over,
Night is drawing nigh,
Shadows of the evening
Steal across the sky.

. . . .
Jesus give the weary
Calm and sweet repose,
With thy tenderest blessing
May our eyelids close.

Grant to little children
Visions bright of thee,
Guard the sailors tossing
On the deep blue sea.

Through the long night-watches
May thy angels spread
Their white wings above me,
Watching round my bed.

When the morning wakens,
Then may I arise
Pure and fresh and sinless
In thy holy eyes.

THE DAY WE SAW THE ANGELS
S. Ralph Harlow

It was not Christmas, it was not even wintertime, when the
event occurred that for me threw sudden new light on the
ancient angel tale. It was a glorious spring morning, and my
wife, Marion, and I were walking through the newly budded
birches and maples near Ballardvale, Massachusetts.

Now, I realize that this, like any account of personal experience, is only as valid as the good sense and honesty of the person relating it. What can I say about myself? That I am a scholar who shuns guesswork and admires scientific investigation? That I have an A.B. from Harvard, an M.A. from Columbia, a PH.D. from Hartford Theological Seminary? That I have never been subject to hallucinations? All this is true, and yet I doubt that such credentials can influence the belief of another.

In the long run, each of us must sift what comes to us from others through our own life experience, our view of the universe. And so I will simply tell my story.

The little path on which Marion and I walked that morning was spongy to our steps and we held hands with the sheer delight of life. It was May, and because it was the examination reading period for students at Smith College where I was a professor, we were able to get away for a few days to visit Marion's parents.

We frequently took walks in the country, and we especially loved the spring after a hard New England winter, for it is then that the fields and the woods are radiant with new life. This day we were especially happy and peaceful; we chatted sporadically, with great gaps of satisfying silence between our sentences.

Then from behind us we heard the murmur of muted voices, and I said to Marion, "We have company in the woods this morning."

Marion nodded and turned to look. We saw nothing, but the voices were coming nearer—at a faster pace than we were walking, and we knew that the strangers would soon overtake us. Then we perceived that the sounds were not only behind us but above us, and we looked up.

How can I describe what we felt? Is it possible to tell of the surge of exaltation that ran through us? Is it possible to record this phenomenon in objective accuracy and yet be credible?

For about ten feet above us, and slightly to our left, was a floating group of glorious, beautiful creatures that glowed with spiritual beauty. We stopped and stared as they passed above us.

There were six of them, young beautiful women dressed in flowing white garments and engaged in earnest conversation. If they were aware of our existence they gave no indication of it. Their faces were perfectly clear to us, and one woman, slightly older than the rest, was especially beautiful. Her dark hair was pulled back in what today we would call a ponytail which appeared to be bound at the back of her head. She was talking intently to a younger spirit who looked up into her face.

Neither Marion nor I could understand their words although their voices were clearly heard.

They seemed to float past us, and their graceful motion was as gentle and peaceful as the morning itself. As they passed, their conversation grew fainter until it faded out entirely, and we stood transfixed on the spot, still holding hands. Then we looked at each other, each wondering if the other also had seen.

There was a fallen birch tree beside the path. We sat down on it, and I said, "Marion, what did you see and hear? Tell me exactly."

She knew my intent—to see if I had been the victim of hallucination. And her reply was identical in every respect to what I'd seen and heard.

I have related this story with the same respect for truth as I would on the witness stand. But I know how incredible it sounds.

Perhaps I can claim no more for it than that it has had a deep effect on our own lives. For this experience of over thirty years ago greatly altered our thinking. Once both Marion and I were somewhat skeptical about the absolute accuracy of the details at the birth of Christ. The story, as recorded by St. Luke, tells of an angel appearing to "shepherds abiding in the field" and after the shepherds had been told of the birth, "suddenly there was with the angel a multitude of the heavenly host praising God, and saying, Glory to God in the highest" (Luke 2:8–14).

As a child I accepted this multitude as literal heavenly personages. Then I went through a period when I felt that they were merely symbols injected into a legend. Today, after the experience at Ballardvale, Marion and I are no longer skeptical. We believe that St. Luke records a genuine objective experience told in wonder by those who lived it.

Once, too, we puzzled over the Christian insistence that we have "bodies" other than our normal flesh and blood ones. We were like the doubter of whom St. Paul wrote: "But some man will say, How are the dead raised up? and with what body do they come?" (1 Corinthians 15:35).

In the thirty years since that bright May morning, his answer has rung for us with joyous conviction.

"There are also celestial bodies, and bodies terrestrial: but the glory of the celestial is one, and the glory of the terrestrial is another. . . . So also is the resurrection of the dead. . . . It is sown a natural body; it is raised a spiritual body. There is a natural body, and there is a spiritual body. . . . And as we have borne the image of the earthy, we shall also bear the image of the heavenly"(1 Corinthians 15:40–49).

All of us, I think, hear the angels for a little while at Christmastime. But we reject the very possibility that what the shepherds saw two thousand years ago was part of the reality that presses close every day of our lives.

And yet there is no reason to shrink from this knowledge. Since Marion and I began to be aware of the host of heaven all about us, our lives have been filled with a wonderful hope. Phillips Brooks, the great Episcopal bishop, expressed it beautifully:

"Hold fast to yourself the sympathy and companionship of the unseen worlds. No doubt it is best for us now that they should be unseen. It cultivates in us that higher perception that we call 'faith.' But who can say that the time will not come when, even to those who live here upon earth, the unseen worlds shall no longer be unseen?"

The experience at Ballardvale, added to the convictions of my Christian faith, gives me not only a feeling of assurance about the future, but a sense of adventure toward it too.

THE SNAKEBITE
Debbie Durrance

We had just finished Sunday dinner when our twelve-year-old son, Mark, asked if he and his dog, Bo, could go out into the field beyond our house for a while. "Just be careful," my husband told him. It was the advice Bobby always gave our children whenever they went out alone, especially in the three years since we'd moved thirty miles out into the brushland of southwestern Florida. Several of our animals had been bitten by rattlesnakes.

As I cleared away the dinner dishes, I watched Mark and Bo race off through the orange and lemon trees of our private oasis. Mark had become so self-reliant out here in the country, I thought.

I took my time with the dishes, enjoying the slow Sunday afternoon, and was just finishing up when I heard the living-room door open. Suddenly our older son, Buddy, yelled, "Mark, what's wrong?" I threw down the dish towel and ran toward the living room just as Mark gasped, "I—I've been rattlesnake-bit—" There was a dull thud. When I got there, Mark was on the floor, unconscious. "Go get your dad. Hurry!" I said to Buddy.

I pulled off Mark's shoe; his foot had already swollen into a large, ugly purple mass. There was a musky odor about him, the same odor we'd noticed the times our animals had been bitten by rattlesnakes. In seconds, Bobby rushed in and grabbed Mark up in his arms. "Come on," he said. "We've got to get him to the emergency center."

We ran and climbed into the cab of Bobby's work truck. I held Mark on my lap, Buddy sat in the middle, and Bobby drove. "O God," I prayed, "help us." It was seventeen miles to the emergency center, and every minute counted.

Mark was unconscious, and convulsions jerked his body. I tried to hold him still, with his face close to mine. As long as I could feel his breath against my cheek, I knew he was still alive. But the soft flutters were becoming weaker and less frequent.

"Hurry, Bobby—please hurry!" I pleaded as he frantically passed car after car. Buddy sat in the center, quietly struggling to hold his brother's legs. None of us dared say it, but we all knew we were in a race with death.

As we neared the business section, steam started to seep out from under the hood of the truck. The motor was overheating. About a mile from the clinic, the motor began to pop and sputter.

I glanced over at Bobby. What would we do if the motor stopped? But before I could get the words out, Bobby had to brake for a slower vehicle and the motor cut off completely. I clutched Mark to me, trying to hold on to whatever life was left. We were right in the middle of traffic. Cars were pulling around us and honking their horns. Bobby jumped out and tried to flag down one of the motorists, but the cars just sped around him. "Why won't they stop?" Buddy sighed.

Desperate by now, Bobby ran over and pulled Mark from my arms. He carried him out to the rear of the car, where the other drivers could see him, but still the cars kept going by. Finally one old compact car stopped. The driver appeared to be a Haitian farm worker, and he didn't understand English. But he could tell we needed help.

"Thank you, thank you . . ." Bobby shouted as he pulled open the door and pushed Buddy in the backseat. Then he laid Mark down beside him and waved the driver off as I jumped in the front.

"We have to get to the emergency center" I cried, but the driver's questioning look told me he didn't understand. I pointed in the direction we should go.

As we pulled away, I glanced back at Bobby standing in the street. There was no room for him in the small car and our truck was blocking traffic, but I wished he could be with me.

At the emergency center, medical technicians started working on Mark immediately, trying to stabilize his condition. They started fluids and began artificial respiration. But soon after Bobby arrived, the emergency technicians told us they had done all they could and were transferring Mark to Naples Community Hospital, where Dr. Michael Nycum would meet us.

By the time we arrived at the hospital, Mark had stopped breathing twice and had gone into a coma. For the next twelve hours we waited and prayed while the doctors and nurses worked constantly with him. We could tell by the looks on their faces that they didn't expect him to make it.

"Folks, about the only thing the little fellow has going for him is his heart—and that's under tremendous strain," Dr. Nycum told us.

We watched helplessly during the next twenty-four hours as the venom attacked every part of his body. His eyes swelled so tight that all we could see were the ends of his eyelashes. His leg was so swollen the doctors had to make long slashes along it to relieve the pressure on the blood vessels. And still they were afraid they might have to amputate.

Then, miraculously, Mark passed the crisis point and began to improve a little. He was still in a coma, and certainly not out of danger, but the swelling began to go down.

After that, each day brought improvement. On Thursday, Bobby and I sat there beside Mark's bed. We were drained, exhausted, prayed out. I was sitting in a chair close to him, holding his hand, when I thought I felt a movement. But no, I told myself, it was probably my imagination. Yet a moment later, there it was again, a faint fluttering of the small hand inside mine.

"Bobby," I said, sitting up and reaching across to him, "Bobby! Mark moved—he moved!"

Bobby summoned the nurses and doctor. Mark was coming out of the coma.

"Mom . . . Mom . . ." he moaned.

"Yes, honey, we're here." The words caught in my throat.

"Dad . . ."

"Yes, Son . . ."

His eyes opened now as he looked over at Bobby. "Dad . . . are you mad at me?"

"What do you mean?" Bobby tried to laugh, but it came out a little ragged. "Of course I'm not mad at you."

"I was afraid you'd be mad at me for being so careless."

Bobby reached over and patted Mark on the head. "We're just thankful you're getting better. But what happened, Son? Do you feel like telling us?"

The nurses and Dr. Nycum moved a little closer.

"Well, Bo and I spotted a bird in a cabbage palm and, well, I guess I wasn't paying too much attention to where I was going. I was looking at the bird and jumped over the ditch . . . and my foot landed on something that moved when I hit it.

"And then it was like something slammed down hard on my foot, and my leg started getting real hot. When I looked down, I saw a big rattler had hold of my shoe—it was biting on my foot. It was hurting so bad and Bo was barking and jumping at the snake, but it wouldn't let go. Then Bo jumped on the snake and tore into its head. It let go and crawled off into the bushes.

"Dad, I tried to remember what you said to do if we ever got snakebit, but I was hurting so bad, and getting weak and dizzy. I was a long way from the house, and I knew none of you would hear if I called . . ."

"But where were you, Mark?" Bobby asked.

"Out in the field, a long ways from the house. Out there next to the ditch in the field."

"But that's a third of a mile from the house. How did you get to the house?"

Dr. Nycum shook his head. "Medically speaking, it would have been impossible for him to have walked that far."

Bobby and I looked uncertainly at each other. There were also the thirteen steps up to our front door—he'd had to climb those too. I took a deep breath. After everything that had happened, I was almost afraid to ask, but I had to know, "How did you get back to the house, Mark?"

"Well, I remembered you and Dad saying that the more you moved, the quicker the poison would reach your heart, and I knew I couldn't run. But I was so scared, and all I wanted to do was get home. I probably would have run if I could have, but I couldn't because it hurt so bad. And then . . . Dad, there's something I have to tell you. About the man."

"The man? What man?" Bobby asked. "Was someone out there with you?"

"Yes—I mean, no—I mean, I don't know. All I know is that he carried me . . ."

"He carried you?"

"Yes, when I couldn't make it to the house. He picked me up." I could feel a tingle on the back of my neck.

"He talked to me in a real deep voice," Mark went on, "and told me that I was going to be real sick, but that I'd be all right."

"What did he look like?" I asked Mark shakily.

"I couldn't see his face, Mom. All I could see was that he had on a white robe, and his arms were real strong. He reached down and picked me up. And I was hurting so bad, I just sort of leaned my head over on him. He carried me to the house and up the steps. When he put me down, I held on to the door and turned around, and—"

His blue eyes stared into mine with an earnestness I'd never seen before. "All I could see was his back."

For a long time, none of us could speak; it was almost

more than we could take in. "God is our refuge and strength," I said to myself, "a very present help in trouble" (Psalm 46:1, RSV).

For most of my life I had believed that passage in the Bible by faith. Now I saw the proof of it.

"Mom . . . Dad . . ." Mark said, hesitating. "I know you may not believe me—"

"We believe you," I whispered as Bobby put his arm around me. "We believe you."

 ## THE CONFRONTATION
Mark Richard

I had been in New York just a few weeks, having moved here from Virginia Beach, Virginia. The only apartment I could afford was in a bad neighborhood in the borough of Queens, where at night roaches skittered across the walls and the streets were filled with young toughs. After much prayer and searching, I found a temporary job in a restaurant in Manhattan's Greenwich Village.

The restaurant often closed at two or three in the morning, but because we had to count out the registers and clean up, we waiters were sometimes not able to leave until four. Then I had to cross several dark streets with my tips, all the money I had in the world, divided in different pockets and zippered in the lining of my jacket. The idea was, in case I was mugged, maybe the thieves would not take everything I had. I learned this ploy from my co-workers. While cleaning up, they would often swap tales of being held up on the way home—at knifepoint, gunpoint, or just by a hand thrust into a paper sack (and having to decide whether a weapon was really concealed within). I later learned from a police detective that generally there *is* a gun in the paper sack; muggers use the tactic so victims will not freeze with fear and fail to cooperate.

After leaving the restaurant I would catch the Seventh Avenue subway to Times Square, where I would transfer to the Number 7, the only train out to my neighborhood. At that hour, the Times Square subway station is a strangely quiet place. Long corridors connecting platforms are empty. There are blind turns. Great lengths of walkways are garishly lit with bare bulbs. It is a place of passage for the occasional late-night reveler, a retreat where the homeless sleep. And it is a place for those intent on criminal mischief, for the subways themselves provide getaways, and the tunnels a maze of hiding places.

One night I stood on a platform waiting for a train that seemed long overdue. I had been on my feet for ten hours serving a surly Saturday-evening crowd. At the other end of the platform were three young men. We seemed to be the only people in this place. Indeed, I felt as if we were the only people in this big city waiting underground for a train home.

After a while, I noticed that the three men were watching me. Were they sizing me up? I told myself I was just being paranoid from being tired, having about a hundred dollars in tips in my pockets, and being new to the city. Still, I moved a little way down the platform.

That was probably a mistake. Animals can detect fear in humans, and I am sure that experienced criminals can do the same thing. The three men moved down the platform, easing closer to me. Needless to say, I was whispering some quiet prayers and glancing at a stairway that would be my escape route if I had to make a run for it.

To avoid showing my fear, I concentrated on the tiles in the opposite wall across the subway tracks and looked down the darkened tube, hoping and praying the train would arrive. I became aware of how cavernous the entire structure was; in some ways its arches and ceilings reminded me of some cathedrals I had visited.

The three young men were now watching me closely and taking smaller steps to where I stood. Instead of fearing for my life, incredibly, I was wondering how I was going to pay my rent after being relieved of my money. I took another step toward the stairway leading up from the platform.

At this point I put everything into the Lord's hands. I was praying. I was sweating. In the adrenaline rush of fight-or-flight, I was preparing to run up the stairs when one of the men walked around me to the foot of the stairway, where he stood, arms crossed, staring at me.

Just as I was expecting them to demand my valuables, a

strange thing happened. From the stairway came a singing
voice. It was so soft at first that it could have been just a note of
a distant siren, but then I distinctly heard a couple of phrases.
The song was in a language I did not understand. As the voice
grew louder, it sounded like Latin. It was a soft male voice but
strong and confident in its high reaches.

Our little platform drama halted. In fact, the man from
whom I expected the demand, who only moments before
seemed ready to speak, remained quiet, as if his words stuck in
his throat. The voice approached us from the stairway, and now
we could even hear slow, steady, heavy footsteps. My first
instinct was to thank God for sending me an Irish cop on his
beat singing a song from his days as an altar boy.

Apparently my companions did not share my perception of a
possible rescue. Perhaps it was because the footfalls were taking
so long to come to the top of the stairway. Perhaps it was the
song itself. Perhaps, although the steps sounded heavy, the
voice was so delicate that its owner would be little deterrent to
crime. An arm reached for my jacket.

And there we stood, motionless, everyone, including the
youth with his hand on my sleeve, staring at the stairway.

The singing grew louder; it began to echo down the platform
behind us, reminding me of my cathedral comparison earlier.
How odd, I thought, that such a place could have such wonderful acoustics. That one voice was sounding better and better as
it got closer and closer. I knew that whoever the voice belonged
to would decide my fate for that night, perhaps for my life.

The miracle is, no one appeared at the top of the stairs. No
Irish cop, no late-night reveler, no choir member, no one. The
footfalls came to a stop there and the singing voice was instantly
drowned out. I was just as disturbed as I was relieved.

What drowned out the voice in those final moments was the
approaching roar of my train coming into the station. The
platform filled with people, and then a transit cop disembarked.
I am sure I was saved because the young men were waiting to
discover the identity of the singer with the heavy tread.

I called my mother the next day to tell her about the eerie
happening, and she began to cry. She said that the previous
night she had asked a special prayer—for me to be surrounded
by a legion of angels.

But I knew it wasn't necessary to pray for an entire legion. One with a fine voice and a heavy foot was all I needed.

❄ PRAISE HIM FOR HIS MIGHTY ACTS (AND HIS LESSER ONES, TOO)

Efrem Zimbalist, Jr., as told to Regina Walker McCally

Would you believe four flat tires on one car in one day? Well, listen to this.

Back in 1953 I was planning an easy little trip from my home in Connecticut to Pennsylvania. I had four brand new tires for my car. And that was no ordinary car—it was (and is) the motorized love of my life. It's a 1934 Packard, a tan and chocolate brown beauty, with long sleek lines and highly finished grillwork up front. The top lets down, and there's a sturdy running board on either side of the chassis, which rests on gleaming wire wheels. More about those wheels later.

Life was unsettled for me back at that particular time. Emily McNair, my first wife, had died of cancer. Emily and I had bought that Packard together. It had been an old wreck of a car sold to us by a New Englander with a thick Maine accent.

We had hired a mechanic to restore it, but Emily died before the car was finished. So there I was with our two small children, Nancy, seven, and Efrem III, four. And the Packard.

I withdrew from acting for a while to give myself time to heal, and in the interim I began composing music. I come from a musical family. Mother was a beautiful soprano known on the opera stage as Alma Gluck; and my father, a celebrated violinist and composer, was then director of the Curtis Institute of Music in Philadelphia.

Now *my* first work was going to be performed! It was definitely a thrill, the prospect of going down to Merion, on the Main Line outside of Philadelphia, to hear it presented. I'd written a motet, a choral work sung without instrumental accompaniment. It was based on a sacred text, Psalm 150, an unusual sort of composition for me since I wasn't all that religious. At the time, that is. But I'd put my all into that piece, and it was one of the numbers to be performed on a Sunday afternoon program of religious music by a very distinguished group. My father would be in attendance, too.

The plan that Sunday was for me to drive down to New York, park the Packard, then continue by train to Philadelphia, where I would meet my father. Together we would make the short commute by train to Merion. But if I had known then what awaited me, I might never have ventured out that Sunday. I drove a short distance down Route 202, following the Aspetuck River, then turned off onto Route 37 for a shortcut into New York. There were dark clouds overhead, but the day started off happily.

"Tah, dah, tah, tum, Praise ye the Lord . . . Praise him with the timbrel and dance, dah, dah, dah, dah," I sang, lustily, snatches of my choral work that soon would be magnified by many voices. "Oh, Prai-i-i-se him upo-o-o-on—" *POW!* My left tire. My *new* left tire.

"What in the world?" I exclaimed. "I just *bought* those tires." The flat had come just as I entered the small town of Sherman, Connecticut, and it posed an immediate dilemma for me. There were two spares sitting grandly in the sidewells along the running boards, but they were there mostly for show. They were old and couldn't be trusted. So I ran around trying to find a service station—one open on Sunday. The one I finally found had to call Litchfield, twenty-two miles away, and have a tire delivered.

Well, I figured, *that's okay*. I'd allowed an extra hour and a half traveling time.

Annoyed over the delay but glad that I'd started out early, I drove the Packard back onto the highway. "That tire shouldn't have blown. What bad luck," I brooded. Soon, though, I was humming to myself and fantasizing about the reception I'd get for my motet.

"Praise him with the sound of the trumpet: praise him with the psaltery and harp . . ." *HONK! HONK!* Someone waved at the Packard. (The Packard always gets a lot of attention.)

The dark clouds had now opened up, and rain pelted down. Then I heard a second *Pfffft, flop, flop*. My right rear tire!

"This *can't* be happening!" I said out loud. There I was, in the middle of a downpour on the Saw Mill River Parkway. Straining under the Packard's weight, I began jacking up the car; but the jack broke and splattered me with mud. My temper smoldered.

With good leather shoes sinking in the ooze, I tromped off to find a farmhouse and a phone. A wary woman answered my knock. Through the cracked door, she stared suspiciously at my wet suit, the hair plastered to my forehead, the splotches of mud on my face and clothes.

"Strangers ain't allowed here," she said brusquely. *Slam* went the door. *Click* went the latch. Precious time was lost as I persuaded her through the door to call a service station to come and fix my flat. By this time my head start had eroded.

The tire changed, I was back at the wheel, sitting damply on the leather seat, spinning down the Saw Mill, trying desperately to make up for lost time. And then, the third tire went. The Packard limped into a nearby service station.

Through clenched teeth, I called my father in Philadelphia and told him to go on to the concert without me. I would meet him as soon as I could get there. Dad tried to soothe me, but it was no use.

Back in the car, my blood pressure was boiling. My moment of triumph had been lost, all because of those miserable tires. I no longer puzzled over the oddity of their going flat. I was too infuriated.

And so, when the fourth one blew, I was a dangerous man. I banged shut the door of the Packard. Not even the rain could cool me off. And where was I this time? On the Henry Hudson Parkway. I could *see* the city, but I couldn't get to it. Cars whizzed past, barely missing the Packard, parked precariously on the shoulder just at the end of a curve. No one stopped to help; people only honked and yelled warnings and shook their fists.

But I was too angry to give up. I was going to complete this trip if it killed me! Then I heard it, a *chug-chug-sputter-sputter*, and a jalopy, driven by an old white-haired man, pulled up behind me. Off went the engine, and the man's head slumped against the steering wheel.

Minutes passed, nothing happened. Still seething, I stomped over to the old car and asked gruffly through the window: "Hey, what are you doing here?"

When the old fellow looked up, I caught my breath. I hadn't expected the serene, compassionate gaze that met my angry glare. His face was almost, well, beautiful; and although he must have been near eighty, his eyes seemed ageless.

In a feeble voice, with frequent pauses, he explained, "I'm a little tired, and I thought I'd take a rest."

"A rest!" I yelled. "On the Henry Hudson Parkway?" Could this man be pulling my leg? I wondered. I was beginning to think I was going gaga.

"And what are *you* doing here?" the old man asked in a singsong voice.

"I have a flat tire," I snapped. "In fact, it's my fourth flat tire of the day!"

No reply. Then, after a long wait, he said, "There's a garage a mile and a half down, at the next exit. They'll fix it."

"Don't you understand," I fumed, "I have a flat. I can't drive that far on the rim!" Why, I wondered, was I standing here in the rain talking to this old guy?

After another minute's pause, he asked, "Then why don't *you* fix it?"

I wanted to shake this man until his teeth rattled, I was so mad. "Because my jack broke!" I replied, exasperated by this slow-motion conversation.

Looking at my mud-spattered watch, I realized that the concert would be starting soon.

"I have a jack," said the old man, and he handed me the keys to his trunk.

"Why didn't you say so in the first place?" I said huffily, as I got the jack. As quickly as I could, I changed the tire, then returned the man's jack and keys. Neither of us spoke.

I went back to the Packard, whacked on the hubcap. Then, feeling guilty about my rudeness, I turned back to thank the old gentleman. And I gasped! Jalopy and man had vanished. Without a *sound*. I remembered the sputtering of his engine when he pulled up behind me. There was no way to sneak off in *that* car.

I ran up the Parkway and looked into the distance, cars zooming and screeching around me. No trace of him. "I *am* losing my mind," I said out loud.

Then I began to wonder. Was that man real or wasn't he? The spare tire in place on the front of my car was proof that he'd lent me a jack. But he couldn't have disappeared in those few seconds—twenty at the most—while my back was turned. It was weird. I felt a shiver down my spine.

On the train ride down to Philadelphia, I continued to puzzle over the old man. *Of course*, I thought, *if it hadn't been for him, I'd still be standing helplessly on the Parkway. But on the other hand, he wasn't all that helpful. He didn't do anything, in fact, until I told him point-blank what I needed. And yet, he gave it—a jack, that's all I needed. And then he disappeared. Just who was he?*

All those flats, I later found out, occurred because the mechanic failed to put on the boots with the Packard's new tires. The boots would have protected the tires from the Packard's spoked wheels.

But, you know, I never forgot that old man, and years later, when I drew closer to God, I felt—and I believe now—that that old man was sent to help me. As exasperating as he was, he gave me the help I needed. But he made me ask for it.

"Ask, and it shall be given you; seek, and ye shall find." (Matthew 7:7).

But wait, there's more to the story of that day. I walked into the concert in Merion, *two hours* late, just as the choral group burst into "Praise ye the Lord . . . Praise him for his mighty acts . . . " The 150th Psalm—*my* motet! Knowing I was delayed, the conductor pushed it back on the program until he felt he could not hold off any longer; and at that moment, I pushed wearily through the doors.

I sat there, muddy and wet, and listened humbly, as the choir's voice swelled at the end: "Let everything that hath breath praise the Lord. Praise ye the Lord."

❄ FOOTPRINTS IN THE SNOW
Sandy Seltzer

Dustin, my California-bred guide dog, was having trouble outside our Long Island apartment. This was his first snowstorm and he was confused. I'm blind, and I wasn't doing so well either. No one was out, so there were no sounds to steer me. Contrary to what many people think, guide dogs do not find the way for a blind person. The blind person directs the dog.

After a harrowing forty-five minutes, Dustin and I finally made it back. But guide dogs must be walked regularly. "Next time why don't you ask God to go with you?" a friend suggested. And so I did. "Lord, go with Dustin and me. The wind is so fierce it's hard to concentrate on our direction. Lead us."

Snow stung our faces and it was difficult to make a path. Dustin whined a little. "Okay, boy," I said to him, "the Lord is with us." And then I gave him a command that a blind person gives only when another person is leading the way: "Dustin, follow!"

Dustin perked up and to my astonishment took off as though he knew exactly where to go. We made it to the street, then headed back to our building—no problem.

A young woman trudged up and offered to walk us to our door. "We'll just follow your footprints," she said. "Yours and the dog's, and that other person's."

"What other person?" I asked.

"There's a dog's prints. And your prints. And a larger person's prints. Wasn't someone with you?"

I paused for a moment and then I answered, "Oh yes, there was Someone with us." There always is.

STRANGE ENCOUNTERS
Kimetha Brown

I was exhausted, numb with grief and shock and fear. The last twenty-four hours had been an unceasing nightmare. I didn't see how God could permit such things to happen to anyone, let alone my little boy, David. I didn't know whether he would survive; the doctors said they couldn't tell me. I didn't know whether the mountain lion that had mauled him was rabid or not. I stood in the hospital corridor and turned my face to the wall and wept silent tears of hopelessness and despair.

Then, although I had heard no one come up behind me, I felt a pair of loving arms enfold me—gentle, supportive, understanding arms. I thought it must be my husband, Chris. Or perhaps some friend or relative who had heard about our trouble and had hurried to the hospital.

But it was not my husband. It was not a friend. It was someone I had never seen before.

And would never see again . . .

The unbelievable had happened the previous day on a rocky trail in Big Bend National Park on the Texas side of the Mexican border. It was a scorching afternoon, August 2, 1984. As my two sons, David, eight, and Justin, four, raced ahead of us, their stepfather, Chris, called them back, reminding them that the park rangers had told us to stick together. They had said that these piñon-juniper woodlands hid coyote, white-tailed deer, javelina, desert mule, even some mountain lions that occasionally were seen at a distance. But no one had ever been threatened by these. The thing to watch out for on the path we were taking, they said, was snakes.

Suddenly, David swung around, his face contorted with fear. He ran toward us screaming, "Mountain lion!"

Before any of us could react, a cougar sprang from the shadow of a tree. Like a tawny streak of lightning it pounced on David's back. The next moment he lay sprawled, not moving, as the huge cat clamped its teeth over his head . . .

There are moments in life that burn themselves into your brain, into your soul. That moment burned into mine. As I stood there in the hospital corridor, I knew it would never go away. And yet, as the gentle arms enfolded me, a soft voice said, "Child, you don't know me. But I know you." I turned and found myself gazing into the face of an elderly black man. He was wearing dark glasses. He wore some kind of old hat. He held a small brown paper bag in one hand, the top crumpled shut. I think—but I'm not absolutely sure of this—he was wearing some sort of brown coveralls.

All this I saw through my tears at a glance. My first reaction was one of astonishment, resistance, almost fright. He must have felt me stiffen, because he said soothingly, "I know all about you and why you are here. God knows too."

I heard these words with incredulity. How could he know about me? No newspaper had published the story. There hadn't been time. And yet, startled and incredulous though I was, I was aware that something remarkable was happening. I have a normal wariness of strangers, but in an instant, it seemed, something melted away that resistance. I no longer felt afraid. I just felt loved. I yielded to the comfort of this stranger's arms. And cried . . .

When the cougar pounced, I watched in horror, unable to move or make a sound. But Chris burst into action. He hurled himself at the lion, trying to kick it away from David. The beast writhed in pain and anger, but did not release its hold on the child. Chris slipped and fell almost on top of them. I screamed, "He's killing him! He's killing him!" Chris seized the cougar by the neck, trying to choke it. Justin was running in circles like a mad thing. When I snatched him to me, he climbed all over me, half crazed with fear. I wanted to calm him, but I couldn't stop screaming.

With colossal effort, Chris wrenched the cougar away from David and flung it aside, but the enraged beast came right back, sinking its claws into his leg. With his free foot, Chris kicked with all his might and the cougar flew backward. Chris snatched up a tiny stick and lunged at the lion with a furious yell. The bluff—and what a courageous bluff it was—worked. The animal sprang into the underbrush and disappeared.

Chris scooped David up in his arms. David's eyes were open but filled with blood. His skull lay exposed; parts of his scalp hung in shreds, bleeding terribly. There were tooth and claw marks all over the upper part of his body. But he was alive.

"Got to stay together!" Chris gasped at me. "Thing might come back!" He tried to hoist David onto his back, but our son was too weak to hold on. So Chris carried him in his arms. After about fifty yards he stopped long enough to rip off his shirt and wrap it tightly around David's head. Then we ran together back toward the lodge and help. But it was more than half an hour away. I didn't see how Chris could make it with a seventy-two-pound load of dead weight in his arms. Twice I saw the bushes move on the side of the path. The lion was trailing us.

"Daddy," David murmured weakly, "am I going to die?"

"No, you're not!" Chris assured him. "We're going to pray."
And as we stumbled on, we did pray. Chris thanked God for
sparing David's life. He asked for healing for David, and for
strength for himself to make it back to the lodge. David joined
in, and as they prayed together I saw blood running down
Chris's leg. I couldn't tell if it was David's blood or my
husband's. They both ran together. A short while later, I
remembered a phrase from the Bible where another David said,
"The Lord delivered me from the paw of the lion" (1 Samuel
17:37). I clung to that . . .

*I clung to it just as I was clinging now to my comforting stranger.
He said, "God sent me to tell you that your little boy will be restored."
Restored. What a strange, archaic word, but one with such healing
power in it. And hadn't that other David also used that word in the
loveliest of his songs, "He restoreth my soul . . ."? My own soul was
being restored. The fear and despair were leaving me.*

*Now the old man whose arms held me so securely began to pray in a
low, musical voice, the most beautiful prayer I ever expect to hear this
side of Heaven. He thanked God for saving David's life. He thanked
Him for giving Chris and me the strength we needed. Listening to him,
I was sure that God was listening too. I knew that David was going to
be all right . . .*

When at last we stumbled into the lodge, the horrified
rangers sprang into action. A paramedic treated David's terrible
wounds as best he could. An old park van rushed him to the
nearest hospital in the small town of Alpine 110 miles away.
We prayed together the whole way. There nurses tried to clean
and dress the wounds according to instructions given over the
telephone by a trauma team at the Parkland Hospital in Dallas.
It was imperative that David be rushed to Parkland for spe-
cialized care. The danger was that the exposed skull might dry
out and "die," and thus the brain could be affected.

We tried to get an airplane for the five-hundred-mile trip,
but ran into nothing but delays and frustrations. Finally in
desperation we left in the middle of the night by ambulance and
didn't get to Dallas till the next morning. By then David was
running a fever; the antibiotics he had received didn't seem to
be controlling the infection that had set in. Meanwhile, heli-

copters and dogs were out tracking the cougar. To be safe, David had to begin the painful series of rabies shots on top of everything else. It seemed more than an eight-year-old body should have to endure . . ..

The old man stepped back, his hand still on my arm, and I knew he was about to go. I wanted to ask his name, know how he knew about David, how he knew about our need. But he shook his head and smiled as I formed the first question. "I want you to look at my eyes," he said. He took off the dark glasses. His eyes were white. He was completely blind. "I wanted you to see this," he said, "so that you would understand that God really did send me. Watch!"

He turned and walked unerringly down the long, busy hospital corridor. Straight as an arrow, with no cane to guide him, without touching the walls on either side. He did not bump into anyone or anything. I watched him go, the old hat still on his head, the brown paper bag still clutched in his right hand. He turned a corner and was gone. I never saw him again. And even though I asked around, no one in the hospital knew him—or had even seen him.

Today, a year later, David is almost healed, physically and psychologically. He still has occasional nightmares, but they're less frequent. Two more skin grafts are needed, but his hair has almost covered his scalp now. Doctors are amazed by the rapid progress he is making.

They tracked down the cougar. Small amounts of David's hair and skin were in its stomach, positively identifying it. Surprisingly, tests showed no signs of rabies. No one can guess what made this two-year-old female lion attack. In the fifty years the park has been open, such a thing had never happened before.

And that meeting in the Parkland corridor? If you are invincibly literal-minded I suppose you can choose to believe that the person I met—or the person who came to me—was just some casual visitor to the hospital who had heard about David, and who was remarkably perceptive and kind.

But Chris and I will never believe that. We believe that God heard our prayers and sent one of His messengers, yes, a blind messenger with a funny hat and a brown paper bag, to comfort and strengthen us. We'll believe it forever. And we'll never cease to be thankful.

THE FAR SIDE OF MIDNIGHT
Irene J. Kutz

From the time I was a child my parents taught me to believe in God and to know Him. But as I grew up I learned that knowing God and being a professional Christian do not always keep difficulties or heartbreak away. Indeed, there was one time in my life when I felt that God had deserted me altogether.

It happened during World War II, when I was only twenty. Allen was twenty-one. He was in the artillery, the Timberwolf division. He was a Christian, too, and we pledged our lives together and our love to God.

When Allen went overseas with his division, a part of him stayed with me. We were to be married when he returned. We prayed for an early end to the war.

But then there was the Battle of the Bulge. Allen did not come through it.

Words cannot express the agony I felt. From the beginning, from the first time we met, our lives had been so intertwined I had felt that there could be no life for me if his ceased. I could not see how a loving God could permit such sorrow to come to me.

The night I learned of Allen's death was one of heavy, gloomy rain. Unable to talk to anyone, I put on my slicker and hat, and went out to walk in the downpour, trying to escape the unbearable loss, the despair. But they stayed with me.

I don't know how long I walked, or where I went, but finally I found myself on the bridge over the river that flowed through our town, an old-fashioned drawbridge with a bridge-tender who stayed in a little house on the main span, raising the center section when boats came by. I knew he was there, but I was sure that he would not be able to see me in the darkness and the rain.

I leaned over the railing and gazed down into the churning water below, just barely visible by the lights of the town. I had always lived for God, trying to do His will, and now He had betrayed me. If I could just slip over the side into the dark water, oh, the blissful oblivion, the release from pain. The agony of drowning would be over in moments—nothing compared to the torment now tearing me apart. *Oh, Allen, I thought, Allen, Allen . . .*

I heard no sound, but suddenly I felt a hand on my arm. "Come in out of the rain," the bridge-tender said quietly. Numbly I let him lead me to his tiny house on the bridge. He sat me down on one of the two chairs, and poured a cup of coffee from his thermos. Pain possessed me, consumed me. I felt as if I *were* pain.

"It's a nasty night to be out," he remarked. He had removed his slicker, and I did not recognize him as one of the regular men. He was a little man, with an ageless face, and his eyes—the bluest, deepest-set I had ever seen—were compassionate and kind. I had never seen him before, but I felt his spirit touching mine.

I began to cry, and he sat there, across the little table from me, saying nothing. Oddly, his silence didn't seem strange to me; he did not seem like a stranger.

A boat's whistle hooted three times down the river. The man set in motion the huge mechanism that raised the bridge. The boat passed through, and the bridge settled back into place.

My sobbing had quieted, and I found myself telling him about Allen, spilling out my soul as if I'd known him all my life. When I finished, I felt drained, exhausted, but the unbearable knife-edge sharpness was gone.

His eyes stayed on my face as he said quietly, "I can understand your grief." Then he took both my hands in his. "Father," he murmured, "come to Your child."

He bowed his head in silent prayer for several minutes. Then he raised it. "Come now. I'll walk with you to the end of the bridge. The Lord will see you through this. Remember that."

I walked home. I still grieved, but the awful despair was alleviated. I knew somehow that God had not forsaken me. I felt I was no longer alone.

Several days later, I walked down to the river to tell the bridge-tender that I was slowly learning to live with my loss, and to thank him. But he wasn't there.

I described him to the man on duty.

"I don't know who you're talking about, Miss, and I know all the tenders," he told me.

"But the night it rained so hard . . ." I persisted.

"I'm sorry. I don't know who was on duty that night."
I never found out who that man was, and I know I never will.
But I do know Who sent him to me.

THE ORANGE PICKUP
Mary Pettit Holmes

I had to stay late that evening at the bloodmobile, where I am a
registered nurse working with the American Red Cross. By the
time I trudged out to my car, it was dark, and fog was rolling
in. I had an hour's drive home to our small town nestled near
the base of the Oregon coastal range.

The traffic was light, which was good, because the fog was
getting heavier. I could barely see the white line at the edge of
the freeway and the streetlamps that lit it. Then I turned off
onto our country road. Ten more miles to drive on a narrow,
twisting road with deep ditches and a stream alongside.

"Help me, Lord," I prayed. Recently in church we had been
discussing the use of mental imaging while praying. Now I
visualized Jesus sitting next to me in the passenger seat. I
poured out my fears to Him.

Hugging the steering wheel, I stared at the eerie whiteness.
Suddenly ahead of me I saw the red taillights of another car.
Slowly I drew closer. The red taillights were on an orange
pickup being hauled by a tow truck. I was relieved. Undoubt-
edly the pickup was being taken to the garage in Forest Grove.
If I followed it, I could make it home.

We came to Main Street—but we passed the repair shop. The
tow truck drove on. It kept going. To my amazement, it turned
into the dead-end road where we lived. With a sigh of relief I
turned into our driveway, then quickly got out to thank the
driver of the tow truck that had led me home.

There was no driver. There was no tow truck. It had not
turned around to exit from the dead end. I stood staring into the
silent fog at the end of our road.

THE MAN IN THE TREE
Delta Ralls

"Wake up! Water's rising fast!" Somebody was pounding hard on the door of our camper.

When my husband, Earl, and I first fell asleep, rain was hammering on our metal roof like machine-gun fire. Now it was pretty close to midnight, and a ranger outside was hollering that people should move their boats in to shelter.

It was Wednesday, May 27, 1987, and we'd been fishing and camping with some relatives at Chisholm Trail Ridge on Waurika Lake, about twelve miles from where we lived in Comanche, Oklahoma.

By the time I pulled on my jogging pants, Earl had disappeared into the downpour. But in a minute he came back, holding up half a boat key. "Broke off in the ignition," he yelled.

"I'll go for the spare," I yelled back. We had another key at home, and it seemed easy enough to go get it.

I climbed into our yellow pickup and took off, the windshield wipers flapping away but not helping much. I followed the road along the shore, the pickup bouncing over the ruts. Lightning flashed, and in the eerie blue-white light, trees were bent over and the tall grass was almost flattened by the wind.

I pulled into our driveway, grabbed up the boat key, and headed back around the lake, past Beaver Creek bottom.

By now the storm was even worse. I jounced along over potholes, hoping I was still on the road, when . . .

The pickup lurched, then reeled out of control. Something smashed into the pickup and sent it hurtling through the air. I held on to the steering wheel as hard as I could. Then the pickup dropped with a thud. Icy water poured in everywhere. I threw myself against the door, pushed it open, and fell into churning water that sucked me into the darkness.

Lord help me. I can't swim. I couldn't get my breath. Water stung my eyes, my nose, my throat. I flailed desperately for something, anything, to hold on to.

The water roared like a freight train in a tunnel.

A tree branch! I grabbed it with both hands. The force of the water whipped me around the tree, but I held on. I wrapped my legs around the tree trunk and groped in the darkness for a branch strong enough to climb onto. There! A branch! I hauled myself up and clung to it, shaking.

This couldn't be happening to me—alone. I wanted to cry out for Earl.

Earl! I loved my husband—and totally relied on him. I always had, ever since I came home from the first grade in a one-room schoolhouse in Sugden, Oklahoma, and told Mama I'd be marrying Earl Ralls. Ever since then, when things went wrong, Earl was beside me. I was shy and scared of folks, so Earl always took care of things, protected me.

This time it was just me. And God.

But what a time finally to be thinking of God: when I was in trouble! Why hadn't I been a better Christian? My faith had never wavered, but over the past five years my church attendance hadn't been too regular.

I figured if you were fifty-one years old, unable to swim, sitting in a tree in the middle of the night during a flood, you'd better be prayed up.

I wasn't.

Would God hear me anyhow? I bowed my head against the driving rain and asked for His help.

There was nothing to do now except hold tight and wait. But the rushing water was creeping over my feet and up my legs.

When I was ten, a bunch of us kids were on the lake holding on to the back of a boat, when I got a cramp and had to let go. I'll never forget that feeling of terror as water filled my nose and throat. But Earl's strong arm pulled me out of the water and saved my life. I never did learn to swim, but I learned I could always depend on Earl Ralls.

But Earl wasn't here to tell me what to do in this darkness. Panic-stricken, I reached up for a limb above me . . .

"Don't climb higher until morning."

Was I hearing things? Where did those words come from? I was too terrified to question. I sank back and huddled against the trunk of the tree.

Hour after hour, I held on while the flood roared around me. Gradually light filtered through black clouds. Morning. The water was up to my waist.

I looked up. The branch I'd reached for in the night was

dead. It would have cracked under my weight. The strange command I'd heard last night had kept me from falling into the swirling black water. *God, thank You.*

This time I tested each branch beforehand. Little by little I climbed higher. I scanned the horizon for a boat, rooftop, or any sign of life. But only treetops swayed in the rushing flood. There was no sign of my pickup. I opened my mouth to scream for help.

"Save your strength. Don't yell unless you hear something."

Was someone really speaking to me? Or was I imagining those words? I clung to the tree silently.

More hours went by. By now I was desperately thirsty. I tried to sip a handful of the water surging around me, but the flood had washed manure-spotted pastures, flushed out septic tanks, and carried off the carcasses of dead animals. I gagged.

"Lord," I said out loud, "I'm thirsty."

"Suck your shirt."

I looked around in astonishment. And then down at my T-shirt. I lowered my head, gathered the fabric into my mouth, and sucked out fresh rainwater.

The light faded and the temperature dropped. Thursday evening! Could I stand another night shivering in the darkness? Could I stay awake? Or be able to hold on? My fingers were raw and bloody from clutching the rough bark. I was exhausted, limp, and weak. But worst of all, I was lonely.

I blinked, then blinked again.

Sitting on the branch across from me was the largest man I'd ever seen.

I shut my eyes tight, then opened them slowly.

He was still there. Even in the gathering dusk, I could see his eyes clearly. They were incredibly kind.

Neither of us said a word. His presence radiated warmth and comfort. My shivering stopped; I was enveloped in a cocoon of peace. It was like being in a chapel. For the first time, I relaxed and rested.

The hours passed.

At last the man spoke. His voice was gentle but full of authority. "I'm leaving now," he said. "Don't be afraid; I'm going to bring help."

"Don't go!" I begged. "The water's too rough."

"I'm strong," he said. "Don't worry. Everything will be all right."

He disappeared into the darkness as suddenly as he had come.

Soon it was close to dawn. A bone-chilling wind blew up and whipped the rain into a stinging spray. "Lord, I'm so cold!" I said. And at that moment my body warmed. I felt as though I were being enveloped in a soft, warm blanket. I could almost touch it. I stared at my bare arms in astonishment. There was nothing over them. And yet I actually felt cozy, and my shivering stopped.

Friday morning. I couldn't believe I was still holding on. But who was ever going to find me here? Where was the mysterious man? He hadn't come back.

In a flash it hit me. That man wasn't human! But I knew I hadn't imagined him. He'd been there, talked to me. "I'm going to bring help," he had said.

Could he have been an angel? I'd read about them in the Bible. They were called messengers.

But now I was getting weaker. I couldn't hold on much longer. The water was up to my waist again and still rising. I climbed the last few feet to the top of the tree. Then came the voice again.

"Call for help now."

By now I didn't even wonder if it was real or not. "Help!" I shouted as loud as I could. My voice cracked. "Help!"

Only silence. The water was creeping past my waist now, up and up.

Death. So this was it. Then why wasn't I afraid? All I could think of was the warm blanket that had covered me during the night, and the stranger who had brought me such peace. I closed my eyes.

Voices! Voices not there right beside me but away in the distance. Voices coming closer and closer. I screamed with all my might.

"Wave!" someone out there called. "Wave so we can see you!"

Out of the haze came a small boat rowed by two men.

I woke up between clean white hospital sheets at Duncan Regional Hospital with Earl sitting right beside me, smiling and holding my hand hard. The rest of my family was there too,

and Bob Waitman, pastor of the Patterson Avenue Baptist Church. They told me dozens of people had been over at the church praying that I'd be safe.

Earl and the others had been searching around the Dry Creek bottomland, but I'd been much farther to the west. "You were close to the Youngblood place," Earl told me. "The Youngblood kids went looking for their missing horse and found it in an orchard feeding on some peaches. You must have yelled at just the right moment, because they heard you and ran home, and Mrs. Youngblood radioed for help."

A nurse was turning away folks who had flocked to see me. Earl had told her how shy and scared of people I was, so everybody was surprised when I sat up and said, "Let them in!"

People I'd known all my life, and people I'd never spoken to, put their arms around me; some of them cried. Everybody was amazed at how well I had held up. But I told them, "Don't be thinking I'm Superwoman at fifty-one years of age! The Lord was with me."

For certain, the Lord *had* been with me. And so had that mysterious man. I didn't tell anyone about him then, yet I believe he was an angel.

I'm not so scared of being "out in the world" now. I have a kind of confidence and trust that I didn't have before.

Because I know now that God is always there when I need Him.

His arm is even longer than Earl's.